Table of Contents

Thank you to our contributors

Otto Helweg, Contributing Photographer, www.ottomatic.com

Casey Woods Maddeaux, Contributing Photographer, www.caseywoods.com

Shanti Matulewski, Contributing Photographer, www.vanityfire.com

Rick McConn, Endorsement & Support, roundtop-marburger.com

Diane Mueller, Contributing Photographer, www.dianemuellerphoto.com

Alina Prax, Contributing Photographer, www.ladolcevitaphoto.com

Suzi Q, Contributing Photographer, www.qweddings.com

Deb Taylor, Contributing Photographer, debdiditphotography.blogspot.com

Monica Thomas, Graphic Design & Production, www.tlcgraphics.com

Lina Tran, Project Assistance, longhorn.lina@gmail.com

Emma Lee Turney, Foreword, www.roundtopfolkartfair.com

OTHER PHOTOGRAPHY CREDITS

Photographs for the following companies and events were provided by the following professional photographers:

The Flower Company: Brittany Dawson, www.brittanydawsonphotoblog.com

Deborah Bradley Events: Rae Wells, www.raewells.com

Shakespeare at Winedale: Mark Metts

4th of July Parade: Mark Moran

Sgovio: Paritosho, www.paritosho.com

Emma Lee Turney in Foreword: Glenda Lippman, glenlipp65@aol.com

In addition, The Belle of Round Top, Elisa's Sunday Haus, Junk Gypsy, Round Top Real Estate, Round Top Soap Company, The Shelby, Sterling McCall Antiques Showcase & Events Center, and Wellspring Retreat and B&B provided some or all of their own photography.

FOREWORD

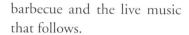

When Hazel Ledbetter first approached me about presenting an Antiques Show at Round Top, I thought … what a great opportunity for our customers and exhibitors to be able to rub shoulders with Texas philanthropist Ima Hogg and restorationist Faith Bybee. Both of these ladies were pioneering collectors and had influenced the preservation of antiques, art and properties nationwide.

The Original Round Top Antiques Fair, held in 1968 in the Rifle Hall, had 22 exhibitors and thousands of Houstonians in attendance. Today, it is owned and managed by Susan and Bo Franks — and held in parallel with antiques shows at myriad other venues in Fayette County! And from that beginning the town has evolved into a weekend destination for both Texans and out-of-state visitors.

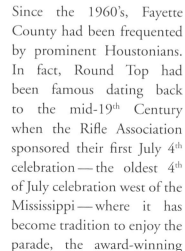

Since the 1960's, Fayette County had been frequented by prominent Houstonians. In fact, Round Top had been famous dating back to the mid-19th Century when the Rifle Association sponsored their first July 4th celebration — the oldest 4th of July celebration west of the Mississippi — where it has become tradition to enjoy the parade, the award-winning barbecue and the live music that follows.

It doesn't take long to see why Round Top is the "Rural Cultural Center of Texas." The Round Top Festival Institute, under the direction of maestro James Dick, is world-renowned as a top classical music center. Winedale Historical Center, a gift from philanthropist Ima Hogg, presents seminars and conferences year-round and hosts the Shakespeare at Winedale series. Henkel Square, a restoration project of Faith Bybee, preserves the Germanic architecture and culture of the founding fathers of the area.

About every 15 years a progressive personality comes to Round Top and opens new, visionary areas. When real estate broker Sandy Reed moved to Round Top in the 1980's, she started the Chamber of Commerce and brought another group of writers. Jacquelyn Ditsler developed Bybee Square, with its art galleries and other fine shops. Leah Hopkins' block, the Village Green, houses Scotty's Restaurant and several small, restored cottages that are now filled with antiques dealers.

(continued on the next page)

And let's not forget Rick McConn, along with his business partner Ashley Ferguson, who have raised the bar as the new owners of Marburger Farm Antique Show.

As a weekend destination, what town with a population of 77 can boast all of this plus three restaurants — Klump's, Scotty's and Royers Café — often featured on national television and in print? In addition, overnight accommodations abound. Your stay might be in a restored 19th Century cottage — your treatment as a guest is the very best!

In this book you will enjoy reading about some of the locations that bring visitors to Round Top, Texas. And once you have visited, your next step is to buy a piece of property or a business from either Round Top Real Estate or Heritage Country Properties to make your name a national identity along with Round Top!"

EMMA LEE TURNEY, November 2009

Emma Lee Turney has a long history, dating back to 1959, producing and managing antiques shows. She is a frequent author and publisher of articles and books on the topic — including *Denim & Diamonds: The Story of the Round Top Antiques Fairs* — and her productions have been featured in major magazines, newspapers and television shows. In the late 1960's, Turney started restoring mid-19th Century Texas houses near Round Top. In 1968, she founded the original Round Top Antiques Fairs. In 2005, she sold

the business to Bo and Susan Franks but retained ownership of the Round Top Folk Art Fair and Creative Market, which also hosts shows during Round Top's now-famous Antiques Weeks.

Read more about her at:
www.roundtopfolkartfair.com/Meet Emma Lee Turney.htm

INTRODUCTION TO THE "ROUND TOP EXPERIENCE"

*L*ocated in south-central Texas, Round Top is a hidden gem — known for its small-town charm, events, shops, lodging and dining. To those in-the-know, Round Top is special because of the beauty of its land and its unique cultural heritage.

Round Top is justifiably famous for its twice-annual Antiques Shows — drawing thousands to the small community and surrounding area. Most residents enjoy the excitement and activity of the shows, but want the world to know there is more to Round Top and Fayette County than just antiques.

While Round Top is known as one of the smallest incorporated towns in Texas (population 77 as of this writing, and measuring one square mile), the surrounding region is home to more than 500 residents tucked away in the woods and hills of Fayette County. What we call the "Round Top Experience" might be better thought of as the "Fayette County Experience," because the cultural and entertainment opportunities stretch beyond the tiny town itself.

Come out for the weekend and experience life on a working farm or ranch, take in a musical performance at Sengelmann Hall, the Bugle Boy or the world-renowned Round Top Festival Institute. Drive over to Schulenburg and tour the Painted Churches. Indulge in a little retail therapy in Carmine or La Grange. Embrace the arts in Bybee Square. Or check into one of the many local B&B's and just relax.

No matter what time of year you choose to visit Round Top and surrounding Fayette County, you are sure to find something new and interesting. You are cordially invited to be a part of the "Round Top Experience."

ROUND TOP EVENTS CALENDAR

Round Top has activities nearly year-round. For up-to-date information on the area, check in with the Round Top Area Chamber of Commerce at 979.249.4042 or at www.roundtop.org.

SPRING

March	⁹ Spring Antiques Show, *Round Top and surrounding towns*
	⁹ Best Little Cowboy Gathering in Texas, *La Grange*
April	⁹ Burton Cotton Gin Festival, *Burton*
May	⁹ Rural Art Guild of Texas Art Walk, *Fayetteville*

SUMMER

June	⁹ Summer Antiques Show, *Round Top and surrounding towns*
	⁹ Shakespeare at Winedale (occasional events in off-season)
	⁹ Festival Institute Summer Series (other programs year-round), *Round Top*
July	⁹ 4th of July Celebration, *Round Top*

FALL

September	⁹ Fayette County Fair, Labor Day weekend, *La Grange*
	⁹ Fall Antiques Show, *Round Top and surrounding towns*
October	⁹ Rural Art Guild of Texas Benefit Dinner, *Fayetteville*
November	⁹ Wine Festival, *Round Top*

WINTER

December	⁹ Christmas Parade & Celebration, *Round Top*
	⁹ Christmas Lane of Lights, *Ledbetter*
January	⁹ Chili Cook-Off, *Round Top*
	⁹ Winter Antiques Show, *Round Top and surrounding towns*

Fourth of July

Round Top is famous for its Fourth of July, known as the "longest continuous Fourth of July celebration west of the Mississippi!" The earliest recorded celebration, on the 75th signing of the Declaration of Independence, was documented in a July 16, 1851, article in the *Texas Monument* newspaper.

Early celebrations were kicked-off with the firing of a cannon until 1889 when John George Kaiser, president of the Rifle Association, was fatally injured after the cannon exploded while he inspected it for not firing. For the Bicentennial Celebration in 1976, Mayor Don Nagel had the cannon fragments restored to once again sound the cannon at the start of the parade.

Round Top was often a must-visit destination for politicians making Fourth of July speeches, including many state senators and representatives. In the old days, the dignitaries often traveled miles by train to Ledbetter and then transported to Round Top by stage. Lt. Gov. W. P. Hobby, a frequent guest speaker, made his first public announcement that he would run for the office during a Round Top Fourth of July celebration.

Today the Fourth of July celebration draws crowds of more than 8,000 people to the "population 77" town. The events are co-sponsored by the Round Top Rifle Association and the Round Top Area Chamber of Commerce. Festivities include speeches, a parade featuring war veterans and decorated floats, performances by the Round Top Brass Band and other musical acts, and activities for kids and adults alike. Members of the Rifle Association (or Schützen-Verein), founded in the late 1800s, offer a traditional barbeque after the parade.

For up-to-date information on all events in the Round Top area, always check in with the Round Top Area Chamber of Commerce at 979.249.4042 or at www.roundtop.org.

Historical information courtesy of the Round Top Area Chamber of Commerce, Round Top Historical Society, the *Round Top Register* and *The Austin American-Statesman.*

Wine Festival at Round Top

*2*010 celebrates the 6th Annual Wine Festival at Round Top. Local businesses and the Chamber of Commerce invite you to join the festivities on the first Saturday of November. Start your tour at the Stone Cellar and make your way into Bybee Square for more wine tasting, live entertainment and fun.

For up-to-date information on all events in the Round Top area, always check in with the Round Top Area Chamber of Commerce at 979-249-4042 or at www.roundtop.org.

204 East Mill Street
Round Top, Texas 78954
т. 979.249.3390
т. 979.249.4042
The Stone Cellar & The Round Top
Area Chamber of Commerce

Christmas Parade

In early December, visit downtown Round Top for the annual Christmas Parade around the square. Warm up with hot stew — proceeds benefitting the Round Top Family Library — as you enjoy a local brass band and carolers in period costume. Watch the procession, including a parade of llamas, as you await Santa's arrival atop a fire truck.

While in town, take the Homes & Historic Places tour, sponsored by the Round Top Area Historical Society. And later that afternoon, visit the Round Top Festival Institute for Tchaikovsky's Nutcracker Ballet.

For up-to-date information on all events in the Round Top area, always check in with the Round Top Area Chamber of Commerce at 979.249.4042 or at www.roundtop.org.

Warm Potato Salad

Courtesy of The Cot-n-Coffee at Walhalla

8 medium-sized russet potatoes, scrubbed clean

3 hard-boiled eggs, peeled and finely chopped

½ medium-sized sweet onion, finely chopped

3 ribs celery, finely chopped

¾ c dill relish

3 - 4 Tbsp pimento, if desired

FOR THE DRESSING:

¾ c mayonnaise

1 tsp yellow mustard

3 cloves fresh garlic, minced

1 Tbsp McCormick's brand seasoning salt

- Boil potatoes whole until cooked through and easily pierced with a toothpick.
- While potatoes are cooking, prepare dressing by placing mayonnaise, mustard, minced garlic and seasoning salt in a small bowl, mix thoroughly and set aside.
- Chop the celery, eggs and onion, set aside.
- Drain potatoes and peel while still hot, place into a large bowl.
- Add the celery, eggs, onion, and dill relish, toss gently to mix.
- Add dressing to potato mixture, stir to combine.
- Serve warm or at room temperature.

SERVES 8 -10
as a side dish

HISTORY of ROUND TOP & LOCAL ATTRACTIONS

THE RICH HISTORY OF ROUND TOP & FAYETTE COUNTY

*L*ong before the antiques shows (*the first one was held in 1968*), the development of the Winedale Historical Center (*Ima Hogg started preserving property there in the 1960's*), and the Round Top Festival Institute (*the program launched in 1970 and is celebrating its 40th anniversary this season*), Round Top and Fayette County had already established a legacy in Texas history books.

Fayette County lay within the boundaries of the original Austin Colony—the first legal settlement of American families in Mexican-owned Texas. The land grant was acquired by Stephen F. Austin in 1821, who obtained permission to settle 300 families (the "Old 300") here. The first college in Texas, Rutersville, was established in Fayette County in 1840.

The region is known for its strong German heritage, but the first settlers were actually of Anglo origin and included Ledbetters, Flacks, Taylors, and Townsends, among others. One of the native sons, Joel Robison, fought under Sam Houston at the Battle of San Jacinto in 1836, at which The Republic of Texas established independence from Mexico. Joel was known to have been in the party that captured Mexican General Santa Anna, and as "the only one to treat the general with any kindness," allowed by his knowledge of the Mexican language. In turn, he was presented with a small chest of the general's belongings, including a braided vest with gold buttons. Local tradition for the next 100 years held that a groom would borrow the vest to wear on his wedding day—and when the vest became too tattered to wear, parts of it were pinned to the groom's clothing instead!

In 1842, a group of German aristocrats made their first land purchases in the area, and by the late 1840s the region had "developed a strong German character." Early settlers in the area had planned to build the town a few miles away on Soergel's Hill, but the route of the main stage line from Houston to Austin ultimately dictated the current location of the town center. Instead, Round Top got its name from the big, white octagonal house on that hill that had a "round top" on its tower, and was visible for miles.

The first U.S. postmaster was appointed to Round Top in 1846, and after a brief name change to "Shults Store," the post office was renamed "Round Top" on November 30, 1848. By 1850, the town had a population of 150, "two stores, two blacksmiths, two taverns, a post office, and a line of tri-weekly stages." The town hosted its first-recorded Fourth of July celebration in 1851. Round Top's famous Independence Day celebration now draws thousands to the town and is heralded as the "longest continuous Fourth of July celebration west of the Mississippi."

In the late 1850's the Lutherans organized. Under the leadership of the German Reverend Adam Neuthard, Bethlehem Lutheran church was built in 1866-67. Noted stonemason Carl S. Bauer built the church from locally quarried stone, and Johann Traugott Wandke hand-built the pipe organ from native cedars. Services are still held in the historic building.

After the Civil War the railroad and major highways bypassed the town and life slowed down, allowing the area to retain its heritage and small-town charm. In 1870 Round Top was officially chartered. In 1873, The Round Top Rifle Association, or Schützen-Verein, was organized for the support and encouragement of innocent outdoor sports. Today the group still promotes target and trap shooting — and dancing — and is the chief sponsor, along with the Round Top Area Chamber of Commerce, of the local Fourth of July celebrations.

In 1929 the Do-Your-Duty Club was founded by a group of prominent local women to restore and maintain the public square. The group continues its work today, holding events and funding important community projects.

Restoration efforts were accelerated in the 1960s when Miss Ima Hogg, noted Houston philanthropist, started buying land and restoring historic buildings. She created the Winedale Historical Center, an outdoor museum reflecting early-Texas Anglo and German lifestyles. In 1967 she donated it to the University of Texas as a center for "studies of the ethnic cultures of central Texas." In 1971 Miss Hogg invited Professor Jim Ayers to have his students perform Shakespeare plays on the campus, and the renowned "Shakespeare at Winedale" program was born. The program is now under the direction of James Loehlin, and Professor Ayers hosts an offshoot summer camp for young students called Camp Shakespeare.

During that same era, Faith and Charles Bybee bought the four-acre Edward Henkel homestead in downtown Round Top and

created the Texas Pioneer Arts Foundation in 1968 to "collect, preserve and exhibit the arts and artifacts, antiques, tools and buildings characteristic of the German-Texan culture that flourished in the Round Top area in the 19th Century." The Henkel Square outdoor museum in central Round Top is now the site of many historic buildings of that era.

Also in 1968, Miss Hogg invited James Dick to Round Top, where the internationally recognized pianist played his first local concert in Henkel Square. A few years later, Mr. Dick bought his first few acres and started the Festival Institute, which has since grown into a 100-acre campus with gorgeous grounds and gardens, a 1000-seat concert hall, and many historic buildings. The Institute now hosts a world-renowned professional training program for classical musicians, a concert series, educational forums, conferences and events.

For more information on the history of Round Top and Fayette County, visit the Round Top Area Historical Society near the post office in downtown Round Top or call 979.249.5058.

SOURCES: Round Top Area Historical Society and the Bybee Collection at Round Top Family Library, including *An Early History of Fayette County,* by Leonie Rummel Weyand and Houston Wade, ©1936 by LaGrange Journal.

Round Top Area Chamber of Commerce

102 East Mill Street
P.O. Box 216
Round Top, Texas 78954
T. 979.249.4042
T. 888.368.4783
F. 979.249.2085
info@roundtop.org
www.roundtop.org
Laurie Fisbeck, *Director*

Round Top Family Library

The Round Top Area Chamber of Commerce has approximately 240 members and focuses on promoting Round Top and surrounding Fayette County. We strive to act as a hub of information for the community and provide up-to-date information for visitors and businesses about all that is going on at any given time in Round Top and the surrounding area.

Visit our website at www.roundtop.org or stop by the Chamber office in the center of Round Top for a calendar of events and detailed information on the many attractions. Our website also offers a lodging feature that helps visitors find accommodations at more than 70 local B&B's. We also offer this feature for antiques dealers for the Antiques Shows.

*I*n addition to the unbelievable art, music, shopping, lodging and dining you'll find on the following pages, a trip to Round Top would not be complete without visiting these noted tourist attractions.

Henkel Square, right in the center of Round Top, is a nationally recognized collection of historic local Anglo- and German-American pioneer buildings from the 1800's. *www.texaspioneerarts.com*

Round Top Family Library, off the town square, is housed in a restored historic church with beautiful gardens and a play area, has a full complement of books plus computers with free WiFi for visitors. *www.ilovetoread.org*

Bethlehem Lutheran Church, not far from the library, was built in 1866 by German immigrant stonemason Carl S. Bauer and sons, and features a hand-made cedar organ by Johann Wandke. *www.rtis.com/reg/roundtop/bethchur.htm*

Round Top Area Historical Society, located near the post office, charts the history of the town, its peoples and cultures, and hosts a small museum with educational programs, historic house tours and events.

Henkel Square

Historic Bethlehem Lutheran Church

The "Merry Christmas Bar"

Art Guild of Rural Texas, located in nearby Fayetteville, sponsors annual art walks and events and houses concerts, after-school classes, summer art camps and an art library. *www.artguildtexas.org*

Fayette County Lake, 15 minutes from Round Top, is a power plant lake with a well-deserved reputation for excellent fishing year-round, offering camping and recreational areas.

For a town of only one square mile and a mere 77 or so citizens, there is so much history and culture, so much to do and see, such nice people to meet, and such spectacular scenery, you're bound to enjoy *your* "Round Top Experience."

"WHAT IS THE ONE THING EVERYONE SHOULD DO?"

We asked the locals and antiques dealers for the "must do's" while in Round Top & Fayette County. Here's what they told us:

1. Go to a concert and walk the grounds at Round Top Festival Institute. *Be sure to visit the herb gardens.*

2. Eat at Royers Round Top Café. *Don't forget the pie!*

3. Discover the history of Texas. *Start with a visit to Henkel Square in downtown Round Top.*

4. Enjoy a Shakespeare play on a summer night at The Winedale Historical Center. *Check the schedule for off-season shows as well.*

5. "Shop 'til you drop!" *Meander the local shops in Bybee Square in Round Top or in historic downtown La Grange.*

6. Do a driving tour of the Painted Churches. *Contact the Schulenburg Chamber of Commerce at 866.504.5294 to connect with a tour guide.*

7. Stop for a glass of wine at The Stone Cellar in Round Top or listen to live music at The Bugle Boy in La Grange or Sengelmann Hall in Schulenburg.

8. Tour the Round Top Family Library. *Take a break in its beautiful gardens or take advantage of the free Wifi and computer access.*

9. Watch the sunset in the hayfield behind the historic Bethlehem Lutheran Church. *Check out the handmade organ inside!*

10. Take a drive down unfamiliar country roads and enjoy the beauty and peace of the countryside. *Watch out for longhorns!*

But before you do anything ... ***Turn off your cell phone!***

The Texas Czech Heritage Museum and Cultural Center

The Historic N.W. Faison House

La Grange Area Chamber of Commerce

ℰxperience La Grange, "where the Hill Country begins," and you'll find something for the entire family year-round. Come experience the Outdoors, our History, the Culture, and a variety of Arts, Music and Entertainment. In addition to the attractions pictured here, visit the historic Town Square, Fayette County Courthouse, Fayette Heritage Library & Museum, and Monument Hill / Kreische Brewery state historic sites.

Visit www.lagrangetourism.com, or stop by the Chamber office in the historic Old County Jail, for detailed information about the unique variety of opportunities awaiting you in Fayette County. La Grange Area Chamber of Commerce is a membership organization dedicated to business development, growth, and success in our community.

171 South Main
La Grange, Texas 78945
T. 979.968.5756
F. 979.968.8000
www.lagrangetx.org
www.lagrangetourism.com
Dan Gilmore, *President / CEO*
dan@lagrangetx.org

The La Grange M-K-T (Katy) Railroad Depot

La Grange Chamber in the Old County Jail

Bran Flax Muffins

Courtesy of Heritage Haus Bed & Breakfast

1½ c whole wheat flour

¾ c ground flaxseed meal

¾ c oat bran

1 c brown sugar

2 tsp baking soda

1 tsp baking powder

½ tsp salt

2 tsp cinnamon

½ tsp ground cloves

1½ c finely shredded carrots

2 peeled and shredded Granny Smith apples

1 c raisins

1 c chopped walnuts

¾ c milk

2 beaten eggs

1 tsp vanilla

- Pre-heat oven to 350 degrees.
- Mix dry ingredients in a large bowl.
- Stir in carrots, apples, raisins and nuts.
- Combine milk, eggs and vanilla in separate bowl, pour into dry ingredients.
- Stir until moist. Do not over mix.
- Fill lined muffin cups ¾ full.
- Bake at 350 degrees for 15–20 minutes.

MAKES ABOUT 12 MUFFINS

ARTS & CULTURE

Beth Anderson Fine Art

T. 979.249.5962
c. 713.703.3130
texasart401@aol.com
www.bethandersonart.com

105 Live Oak Street
Round Top, Texas 78954

*B*eth's impressionistic style captures unique perspectives of the red clay roads and black "gumbo" fields of central Texas. Whether it is an old abandoned home, a barn at the end of a long dirt road, or a beautiful white spire atop a church on the hill, Beth brings its beauty and spirit to life on a canvas, to be held for generations. Beth has been painting for 60 years, starting with winning first prize in a program at the Moore College of Art & Design in 1944.

Beth Anderson

Q&A

Q: *What are you known for?*

A: Original oil paintings. Buyers also select her abstract and fun paintings. Her famous "egg ladies," "thistle lady" and "church lady" are found to be an interesting change of pace for the discriminating collector.

Q: *What is your favorite part of the "Round Top Experience"?*

A: The intent of the residents of Round Top is to create the ambience of a small German farming community by retaining the architectural style of the 1860's era. The vision of Faith Bybee was to create a "Williamsburg of the West" to complement that famous site here in Texas.

Copper Shade Tree

т. 979.249.4127
с. 281.507.4594
info@coppershadetree.com
www.coppershadetree.com

206 East Mill Street
Round Top, Texas 78954

Copper Shade Tree, a fine crafts destination located in the heart of Round Top, displays a delightful collection of decorative and functional crafts, all handmade by Texas artisans. In addition, six events are scheduled throughout the year to showcase a wide range of fine craft media. Make plans to visit the gallery, and you just might happen to encounter an artist demonstrating his or her particular craft. Our warm hospitality and atmosphere encourages you to stay a while. It is very easy to become engaged in the art process, especially after hearing the stories about each unique artist.

Debbie & Gerald Tobola

Q&A

Q: *What is your favorite part of the "Round Top Experience"?*

A: Living in Round Top is a wonderful experience in itself. As business owners, it's rewarding to see the amazement in the faces of visitors, when they experience it for the first time. They can't believe the beauty of the area, the great hospitality, the arts, and the great food. For those of us who live and do business here, this is what makes Round Top an experience that is unforgettable.

Q: *What inspired you to start your business?*

A: As a self-taught artist specializing in copper repoussé and chasing techniques, I needed a gallery for my artwork. Round Top was the perfect spot for our dream.

The Gallery at
Round Top & Comforts

т. 979.249.4119
galleryroundtop@aol.com
www.thegalleryatroundtop.com

The Gallery at Round Top
203 East Austin, Round Top, Texas 78954

Comforts
207 East Austin, Round Top, Texas 78954

The Gallery at Round Top specializes in original artwork and fine crafts created by some of the nation's leading artists. Housed in an old barn, the Gallery invites all to leisurely wander and enjoy the artwork. A colorful collection fills the space. Relax and enjoy the colors and textures of masterfully executed artwork. The Gallery offers the opportunity to experience the journey art brings to the soul. Next door, visit Comforts, our gift gallery of original artwork.

Karen Vernon & Ken Muenzenmayer

Q: *What do you specialize in?*

A: Original paintings and drawings, bronze sculptures, original designs in jewelry, handcrafted furniture, weavings, functional handcrafted pottery and blown glass. Each piece reflects our philosophy: "Expect the Quality, Enjoy the Beauty."

Q: *Do you offer any additional services?*

A: The Gallery sponsors workshops in painting, crafts and creativity by nationally known instructors from across the country.

Q: *What inspired you to start your business?*

A: The owners are artists themselves and avidly believe that art is essential to life and health. Bringing art to people's lives is another part of the artist's creative expression.

No. 3

т. 409.656.0923
donnaparker@no3.me
www.no3.me

Highway 954 at Schulle Road
Round Top, Texas 78954
Donna Parker, *Owner*

$\mathcal{N}$o. 3 in the country… A country road in Round Top will lead you to a knowledgeable array of artistic works. Pass through the industrial spiral gates and enter into a world of collected treasures. From primitive to modern, from Texas to Paris, all can be acquired at No. 3. The experience awaits you.

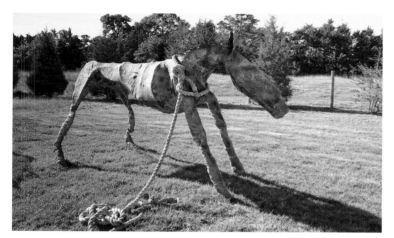

~Q&A~

Q: *What are you known for?*

A: Hip art housed in a vintage 1890's structure. A bit eclectic but oh what fun!

Q: *What else do you want us to know?*

A: Life is a party — not always the one we want, but let's dance anyway. Enjoy Round Top and all that it has to offer!

Q: *Have you received any press recognition?*

A: I have had several homes photographed over the years and the most recent publication featured my Round Top home in *Live Magazine*.

Round Top Festival Institute

T. 979.249.3129
info@festivalhill.org
www.festivalhill.org

248 Jaster Road
Round Top, Texas 78954

Founded in 1971 by concert pianist James Dick, the Round Top Festival Institute is, by now, one of the top summer professional training programs for young gifted classical musicians. The Festival Concert Hall, seating over 1,000, is a unique, strikingly crafted performing venue claiming unmatchable acoustics. The Festival Hill campus (over 200 acres) is open year-round to visitors. It has been generously planted with thousands of trees and bushes of various species. It offers to visitors shadowing lakes, picnic areas, jogging trails and wonderful herb gardens.

James Dick, *Founder & Artistic Director*

-Q&A-

Q: *What inspired you to start your business?*

A: To create a special environment for the arts.

Q: *What is your favorite part of the "Round Top Experience"?*

A: Let's take it from one of our many testimonials: "There is no more welcoming place. I can't think of another classical music venue where everyone is made to feel at home, whether dressed to the nines or in jeans and a T-shirt, all while hearing some of the most talented musicians in the world. And the concerts are just the tip of the ice cream cone!"

LODGING FACILITIES

Overnight accommodations for concerts, retreats, conferences, weddings and other events are available in eight unique buildings on Festival Hill. The forty-four bedrooms include private entrances, heating and air conditioning, full baths and ample dressing rooms.

Mediterranean Garden

THE ROUND TOP MUSIC FESTIVAL & THE "AUGUST-TO-APRIL" SERIES

The Round Top Festival Institute offers a six-week intensive summer training program for young, talented musicians seeking a transition from conservatories and universities to a professional career. Symphony and chamber orchestra, chamber music and solo repertoire are included in the program.

The "August-to-April" Series complements the summer music festival, providing educational forums and music events throughout the year. This series utilizes the variety of resources offered on Festival Hill's campus: performance and listening spaces, library and museum collections, buildings of architectural and historic interest, and gardens.

ANNUAL FORUMS

The Festival Institute presents a number of annual forums throughout the year. These include the Library and Museum Collections Forum, Theatre Forum, Herbal Forum and Poetry Forum. These forums bring highly regarded faculty and enthusiastic participants from across the globe to Festival Hill.

CONFERENCES, WEDDINGS & DINNER ACCOMMODATIONS

The Festival Hill campus is a unique facility set apart from the distractions and frustrations of urban living. The campus includes facilities for weddings, receptions, conferences, retreats, tours (campus and gardens) and photography sittings. Our wedding venue, The Edythe Bates Old Chapel, was built in 1883 in La Grange and moved to Round Top in 1994. The beautifully restored Menke House is available for dinners, rehearsal dinners and wedding receptions. The Edythe Bates Old Chapel and Service Building are both fully equipped for conference presentations.

OUR 40TH ANNIVERSARY

The Round Top Festival Institute 40th Year Project is a coordinated effort to enhance the mission and impact of the Festival Institute by strengthening revenues and expanding the audience size for performances and forums. Rather than only celebrating an anniversary, the goal for the 40th Year Project is to create a solid plan for sustainability for the decades ahead.

Round Top Festival Institute

Sengelmann Hall

т. 979.743.2300
htaylor@sengelmannhall.com
www.sengelmannhall.com

531 North Main Street
Schulenburg, Texas 78956

*S*engelmann Hall is a 19th Century dance hall located in the historical small town of Schulenburg, Texas. Built in 1894 and restored and reopened in 2009, the hall features a restaurant serving a signature blend of Texan and European cuisine influenced by secret family recipes, plus a saloon and biergarten. It also serves as one of the best live-music venues in Texas.

Hana Hillerova Harper & Dana Harper

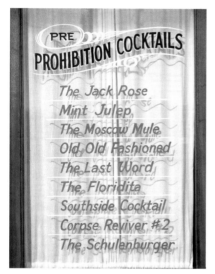

— Q&A —

Q: *What inspired you to start your business?*

A: Texas dance halls are on the verge of extinction. We don't intend on letting that happen! We cherish family entertainment for all ages, which was the inspiration for Dana Harper to restore the dance hall. Sengelmann Hall strives to revive and exude the true essence of the great old halls in central Texas—where people come together to enjoy high-quality food, beverages, and a variety of music and dancing, with a goal of passing down traditions to younger generations.

Shakespeare at Winedale

3738 FM 2714
Round Top, Texas 78954
T. 512.471.4726
www.utexas.edu/cola/progs/winedale
www.cah.utexas.edu/museums/winedale.php
James Loehlin, *Director*

Shakespeare at Winedale is a University of Texas program dedicated to bringing Shakespeare to life through performance. Founded by Professor James B. Ayres on the belief that the best way to study Shakespeare's plays is to perform them, the program offers a unique opportunity to explore these rich and complex texts through the creative act of play. Much of the program is centered at the Winedale Historical Center, where for more than 35 years students and audiences have come to encounter Shakespeare's living art.

Winedale Historical Center, situated on 225 acres near Round Top, is a division of The University of Texas Center for American History that features tours of 19th Century buildings housing early German Texas furniture and decorative art.

Texas Basketball Museum

107 Augsburg Avenue
Carmine, Texas 78932
T. 979.278.4222
T. 800.364.4667
texasbkb@swbell.net
www.texasbasketball.com
Bob Springer, *Founder*

*O*ur museum is the only basketball museum in the state that features the Texas High School Hall of Fame, plus legends of the past from high school to the pros. A huge gathering of basketball memorabilia is on display with items from the sports inception in 1891 through present day. We also have a library of basketball information including the archives of the UIL tournament results.

-Q&A-

Q: *What inspired you to start your business?*

A: Having played for 20 years and coached for 30, it has always been a dream of mine.

Q: *Have you received any press recognition?*

A: We've been covered in *Texas Coach, Street and Smith, The Houston Post, The Houston Chronicle, Basketball Weekly,* the *Fayette County Record* and TABC publications.

Lacey's Buttermilk Pie

Courtesy of Texas Ranch Life

1   prepared pie shell

1⅓ c granulated sugar

3 Tbsp flour

2   eggs, beaten

½ c butter, melted

1 c buttermilk

2 tsp vanilla

- Preheat oven to 400 degrees.
- In medium saucepan melt butter over low heat, add sugar and flour, whisk until mixed.
- Add buttermilk and whisk to blend, remove from heat.
- Mix in beaten eggs and vanilla.
- Pour into unbaked pie shell.
- Bake at 400 degrees for 10 minutes, reduce temperature to 325 degrees and continue baking for an additional 30–35 minutes.
- Allow to cool 15 minutes before cutting and serving.

SERVES 8

DINING

Bistro 108

T. 979.968.9108
info@bistro108.com
www.bistro108.com

108 Main Street
La Grange, Texas 78945
Michael McCathern, *Owner*
Susan Kuehler, *Chef*

*I*magine a small, busy eatery with lots of visiting from table to table … that's Bistro 108. A smile greets you and offers a menu of simply prepared yet flavorful dishes. Featured are locally grown vegetables, choice beef and the freshest seafood available. Our wine list offers excellent wines from Texas, California, Australia and Europe. Bistro 108 is where old friends meet and new friends are made.

-Q&A-

Q: *What special services do you offer?*

A: We cater for weddings, special events and private parties. We also teach cooking classes at the Bistro or in clients' homes and offer a personal chef service.

Q: *What inspired you to start your own business?*

A: We wanted to work together and were looking for an opportunity to slow down. We came to La Grange 11 years ago from Austin. Susan had been in the restaurant business for 25 years and after managing businesses for other people, we decided to open our own restaurant. We haven't looked back since. We have received enormous support from the citizens of Fayette County and beyond. This is a great place to be!

JW's Steakhouse

Jeff Wunderlich

122 South Hauptstrasse
Carmine, Texas 78932
T. 979.278.4240

J W's Steakhouse proudly serves Certified Angus Beef fired over a mesquite grill. We are family-owned and operated, and strive to provide the highest quality and best value, with the warmest service in the business. JW's also has fresh salads, vegetables, gulf seafood, burgers, and delicious homemade cobbler, pies, and cheesecake. We also feature twelve draft beers and an extensive wine selection.

Q&A

Q: Do you offer any special services?

A: We also have the ability to host your private and company parties.

Q: What is the one thing everyone should do while in the Round Top area?

A: Take a drive down the county roads and look at all the beautiful homes.

Oaks Restaurant

5507 Highway 237
Round Top, Texas 78954
T. 979.249.5090
C. 979.249.7217
www.oaksfamilyrestaurant.com
Lori Granum, *Owner*

The Oaks Restaurant has taught me several things. A great restaurant comes together through the hands and minds of all kinds of people. A great food rapport comes from consistency. Great help comes from a working team. And grateful customers come from putting this all together. We're a country restaurant with great food, a homey atmosphere and a friendly staff. We're worth the drive. Promise.

Q&A

Q: *What is your area of expertise?*

A: Our house specialty is baby back ribs and we're also known for our homemade desserts & soups and hometown pizzas. Friday is Fish Fry day and Sunday features peel-and-eat shrimp.

Royers Round Top Café

т. 979.249.3611
pieman@royersroundtopcafe.com
www.royersroundtopcafe.com

105 Main Street
Round Top, Texas 78954

Bud, "The Pie Man" Royer, the funky founding father of Royers Round Top Café, his wife, Dr. Karen, and their four children moved to Round Top in 1987, taking over the tiny 40-seat Round Top Café. The family has built and marketed the café into a well-recognized Texas institution. The story of this iconic Texas bistro has drawn the attention of many regional and national publications.

Bud Royer, Tara Royer-Steele,
Rick Steele & J.B. Royer

-Q&A-

Q: *What's your area of expertise?*

A: The Café's menu isn't the typical country fare but "a Texas country bistro serving gourmet comfort food." They're known for authentic personality, 60's music, the "OMG!" menu, their wine list, and of course, their handmade pies.

Q: *What's unique about your business?*

A: Stepping into the café is an **"ah-ha experience!"** that exceeds your expectations. The quality of the food and service, coupled with the eccentric "stuff" on the walls, along with the 60's music, and "Team Royer"… and you have a an experience that becomes a memory! One well worth the drive!

The Stone Cellar

т. 979.249.3390
tfreer50@aol.com
www.stonecellarwines.com

204 East Mill Street
Round Top, Texas 78954
Terri Freer & Cherie Leighton, *Owners*

The Stone Cellar is a wine shop, pub and pizzeria in a building and cellar built in 1873. Our wine shop is stocked with all of your favorite wines, and our pub features beers from around the world. Our gourmet, thin crust pizza is possibly the best pizza you have ever had!

Justin Klehm & Ryan Willmon

Q&A

Q: *Do you offer any additional services?*

A: We have live music on the patio or in the cellar on most weekend nights. The facility is also available for rehearsal dinners, wedding receptions, fundraisers, birthday parties, etc…

Q: *What inspired you to start your business?*

A: We purchased The Wine Shop, two doors down from our current location. When we saw the charm and history of the cellar, we wanted to move to this location and add a pub and pizzeria.

Lowbrow Meets Highbrow Deviled Eggs

Courtesy of The Round Top Inn

4 eggs

2 Tbsp crème fraiche

1 Tbsp whole grain Dijon mustard

1 Tbsp finely sliced chives

Kosher salt

Freshly ground black pepper

Cayenne pepper

2 Tbsp caviar

- Boil eggs in a pot, about 9 minutes. Drain and peel while still warm. Slice in half lengthwise, remove yolks, reserving whites.

- Place still-warm yolks in a small bowl, and mash with a fork. Add crème fraiche, mustard and chives, and continue mashing until very smooth. Season to taste with salt, pepper and cayenne.

- Using a pastry bag with a small round tip, pipe the mixture into egg halves. Before serving, spoon a little caviar on top of each egg.

SERVES 4
as an appetizer

LODGING

Belle of Round Top B&B

т. 936.521.9300
т. 979.249.4134
belleofroundtop@gmail.com
www.belleofroundtop.com

230 Days End Road
Round Top, Texas 78954
Deborah & Douglas Byers, *Owners*

The Belle of Round Top is housed in a "Jewel of Texas" 1880 Victorian mansion, meticulously restored and decorated with antiques. Guests enjoy warm hospitality, home cooking and beautiful vistas from our verandas. We feature large, comfortable bedrooms with en suite baths, a gift shop with rare collectibles, and WiFi—all within a short stroll to city center. Return to a bygone era for your wedding, family reunion, corporate retreat, or romantic getaway.

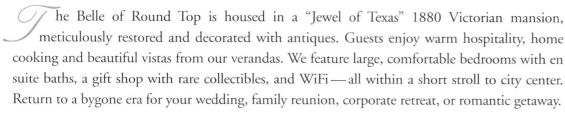

Q&A

Q: *What inspired you to start your business?*

A: This beautiful home represents a period of Texas history that needed to be shared. It was privately owned for 126 years and features incredible craftsmanship using high-quality materials such as cypress, heartpine, 12' ceilings, and etched glass.

Q: *Do you offer any additional services?*

A: The Belle hosts "High Tea" parties, crafting weekends, girlfriend getaways, "elope" weddings, and outdoor "True Texas" weddings with chuck wagon barbeques, plus music from our verandas and dancing under the stars.

The Bootstrap & Silver Spur at Round Top

dloesch@consolidated.net
www.bootstraptexas.com
David & Laura Loesch, *Owners*

The Boostrap: 5100 Roznov Road
Round Top, Texas 78954

The Silver Spur: 7045 FM 954
Round Top, Texas 78954

Our Round Top country guesthouses — located in the heart of the golden triangle of Houston, Austin and San Antonio — are charming yet sophisticated country retreats. They are beautifully restored 1800's traditional Texas farmhouses that provide the comfort and charm of this impressive countryside. They are fast becoming the destination for that special country getaway, offering all the luxury and down-home charm of the ideal escape.

Q&A

Q: *What do you think attracts people to Round Top?*

A: It is such a darling small town with so many things to offer, from its wonderful, unique shops and restaurants to Festival Hill Symphony Hall and the Shakespeare at Winedale program. It has the best of many worlds, packed in a small community.

Q: *What is your favorite part of the "Round Top Experience"?*

A: You feel the warmth from all those wonderful people in town. There is a quaint yet sophisticated feel you just can't miss.

Cot-N-Coffee at Walhalla

T. 281.728.9431
T. 281.813.1960
www.walhallacotncoffee.com

1724 West FM 1291
Round Top, Texas 78954

The Cot-N-Coffee offers a quaint and welcoming getaway for small gatherings, such as family reunions, retreats, weddings, and many other festivities. Close to the Antiques Show, vendors and shoppers find it convenient, affordable lodging. There are five bedrooms that sleep up to 15, a large gathering room, and a full kitchen. Whether enjoying the large front porch that overlooks miles of rolling central Texas, or the screened-in back porch with the fire pit, guests always feel at home in Walhalla.

Belinda & Lynn Warner, Beverly Harper

-Q&A-

Q: *What special services do you offer?*

A: For group catering, we offer barbeque brisket or smoked chicken, as well as fajitas with all the trimmings. And don't miss our homemade, fresh-baked rolls!

Q: *What inspired you to start your business?*

A: The Cot-N-Coffee was inspired by our own wish to have a place for our family to gather and celebrate. It became a pleasure to meet others and to share our home away from home.

Q: *What is your favorite part of the "Round Top Experience"?*

A: As vendors at the Antiques Show for more than 10 years, and now residents of Round Top, it is amazing to see the transformation of the landscape during the Antiques Show. Everyone should visit during and after the show to see the changes!

Elisa's Sunday Haus

599 Bybee Road
Round Top, Texas 78954
т. 832.660.3854
т. 979.249.5522
elisa@roundtopbnb.com
www.roundtopbnb.com

Elisa Henderson, *Innkeeper*

Q&A

Q: *Please share some of the history of your property.*

A: The Ghost Haus dates back to the 1870's. It was inhabited by German-speaking share-croppers but then sat empty for 50 years. During this time local children reported seeing a small, lonely figure in the upstairs window! A descendant of the original owners will host her wedding here in 2010!

Elisa's Sunday Haus and the Ghost Haus, with its vivid history, provide a unique, comfortable and relaxed experience for my guests. Both houses are secluded, quiet and off the beaten path, in a lovely oasis of trees and native plants. A small brook cascading into a pond provides a pleasant sound. With the interior decorations, I remember my ancestors in Germany and honor the German immigrants who came to Texas, beginning in 1840.

Heritage Haus B&B

160 Heritage Street
P.O. Box 284
Carmine, Texas 78932
T. 979.830.7866
heritagehaus@yahoo.com
www.roundtoplodging.com

*D*eb and Matt invite you into their home and treat you like "family." The guestrooms upstairs in this farm-style Texas home built in 1915 are furnished with cozy antiques and personal, handcrafted art collections. They serve a full, hot breakfast using local yard eggs, Burton Market meats, homemade granola, fresh fruits, and house-favorite Bran Flax Muffins loaded with carrots, apples, raisins and walnuts.

Matt Hager & Deb Taylor

Q&A

Q: *Do you offer any special services?*

A: We host Women's Art Retreats such as journal building, jewelry making, knitting and art-doll creating, as featured in *Studios* magazine. We also specialize in story-telling, listening and laughing at the breakfast table!

Meyerland Farm

Pat & Felix Meyer

———— ✦ ————

5696 Wagner Road
Round Top, Texas 78954
T. 979.836.9450
C. 979.251.2575
patmeyer55@hotmail.com

*I*t would be our pleasure to have you stay with us at Meyerland Farm, located about six miles outside Round Top. Fully furnished guest houses or bedrooms upstairs in the main house are available for your enjoyment. You'll savor a full breakfast, usually served on our covered patio. Relax around the firepit or fountain, enjoy the porches and visit with our miniature donkeys and horses.

Oma's Hill Country Cottage

Susan McGee

*T*his charming and relaxing turn-of-the-century cottage rental, located just 15 minutes from Round Top, is filled with antiques and all the comforts of home. It offers three bedrooms, living and dining rooms, a fully stocked kitchen, and a large wrap-around porch complete with rockers. The cottage sits on a secluded acre, has extremely affordable rates and in it you will feel right at home.

Blue House on Main Street
Industry, Texas 78944
T. 832.754.2345
T. 713.973.0566
reservations@omashillcountrycottage.com
www.omashillcountrycottage.com

Outpost @ Cedar Creek Inn

Lincecum Log Home

Lenore Prud'Homme & Danny Riebeling

5808 Wagner Road
Round Top, Texas 78954
т. 979.836.4975
т. 888.433.5791
stay@outpostinn.com
www.outpostinn.com

The Outpost Inn is an award-winning bed-and-breakfast collection of early historic Texas log cabins, cottages and farmhouses, uniquely restored with all the modern conveniences, halfway between Houston and Austin. Our romantic retreat also hosts corporate meetings and weddings. The Outpost won the "Outstanding Inn of the Southwest and West" award by BedandBreakfast.com and is currently listed in the best-seller *1000 Places To See Before You Die — U.S.A. & Canada* by Patricia Schultz. It has also been featured in many publications, such as *Southern Living* and *Cowboys & Indians*.

-Q&A-

Q: *What do you specialize in?*

A: We are a very private and tranquil respite from the big city. We are known for our hospitality and five-star breakfast. We have weekend packages available and will accommodate almost any request.

Q: *What attracts people to Round Top?*

A: Round Top is about as quaint and relaxing as you can get. The town is also synonymous with music, Shakespeare and antiques.

Q: *What inspired you to start your business?*

A: My love of all things domestic.

Pecan Grove Inn

Jane & James Press

233 Augsburg Avenue
Carmine, Texas 78932
T. 281.433.8845
T. 979.278.3965
pecan1@pecangroveinn.com
www.pecangroveinn.com

Come enjoy our lovingly restored 1904 two-story home with a prominent German-style four-gable roof and cozy sitting porch, located on a charming street of other early 1900's homes. We offer two wheelchair-accessible rooms and three upstairs rooms with private baths. Our best feature is our full and varied breakfast each morning! Our many repeat guests come back for more, and more, and more!

Prairie Wind Farm

4507 Havemann Road
Carmine, Texas 78932
T. 979.278.3208
www.pwfarmtexas.com

Linda & Stan Suggs

*P*rairie Wind Farm is a 40-acre working farm with cattle, chickens, and rabbits. Bed-and-breakfast accommodations are provided in guestrooms located on the second floor of the 1921 farmhouse and in an adjacent guesthouse. Fresh eggs, fruits, and vegetables are marketed locally and used in the delicious breakfasts that are always a part of your stay. Children are always welcome.

—Q&A—

Q: *What are you known for?*

A: Guests appreciate our friendly, welcoming atmosphere.

Q: *What inspired you to start your business?*

A: Wanting to share our wonderful old house and lifestyle inspired us to start a bed and breakfast.

Round Top Farms B&B

т. 979.249.3977
c. 281.610.8274
jburger@cvctx.com
www.roundtop.org

301 South Washington Street
Round Top, Texas 78954
Jeannette Burger, *Innkeeper*

ound Top Farms Bed and Breakfast is a two-bedroom, two-bath private house in the heart of Round Top within walking distance of fine restaurants, local historic attractions and great shopping on the town square. One of the most historic homes in Fayette County, this house has beautiful surroundings, antique elegance, and comfortable conveniences to ensure that your stay will be satisfying. Built in 1852 by Carl Siegismund Bauer and given as a wedding present to his daughter Wilhelmine and husband Conrad Schuddenmagen, this house served as the local stagecoach stop where all the immigrants would receive news from Germany.

Q&A

Q: *What inspired you to start your business?*

A: As a realtor in Round Top, I encountered many people new to the Round Top area who expressed a desire to stay in an historic property and experience the charm of this wonderful community.

Q: *Have you received any press recognition?*

A: Round Top Farms Bed and Breakfast has graced the cover of *Texas Highways,* among others, and has been photographed in many publications as a charming, elegant, well-appointed bed and breakfast situated in a beautiful, gently rolling landscape.

Round Top Inn

т. 979.249.5294
info@roundtopinn.com
www.roundtopinn.com

407 South White Street
Round Top, Texas 78954

*R*ound Top Inn, located in the heart of the golden triangle of Houston, Austin and San Antonio, is a charming yet sophisticated historical bed and breakfast. The traditional Texas farmhouses, 1800's restored cottages and Retreat Center are all nestled amongst majestic oak trees and manicured grounds. The Inn is conveniently located three blocks walking distance from unique shopping and restaurants around Round Top's town square.

David Athey

Q&A

Q: *What special packages do you offer?*

A: Unique retreats focused on wellness & fitness, culinary & wine and custom-designed getaways in a tranquil country setting.

Q: *What inspired you to start your business?*

A: After 20 years in the hotel business and experience as a private butler in NYC, I followed my dream of operating an inn while creating a unique lodging experience for guests.

Q: *What is the one thing everyone should do while in Round Top?*

A: Watch the sunset on the hayfield behind the Bethlehem Lutheran Church.

The Shelby

5072 Voelkel Road
Shelby, Texas 78940
T. 214.244.8614
T. 979.277.0200
theshelbyinn@aol.com
www.theshelby.net
Jenifer Jordan, *Owner*

The Shelby was an 1800's town that is now a beautiful bed-and-breakfast and wedding chapel. The Shelby comes complete with an 1830's inn and mercantile, an 1870's school-house, and three Texas farmhouses for lodging. We host weddings in the charming Shelby Wedding Chapel. Guests can plan scrapbooking/quilting retreats, cooking classes, family reunions, spiritual/wellness retreats or just a relaxing weekend. The facility can accommodate large groups of people in the seven unique historical buildings.

-Q&A-

Q: *Do you offer any special services?*

A: The Shelby is pleased to offer a fabulous new cookbook, *Good Things at The Shelby*, containing more than 50 delicious recipes by the notable local chef Kathleen Whatley.

Sommerhus at Warrentop Farm

11630 Schuster Road
Round Top, Texas 78954
т. 512.413.1728
т. 979.249.2750
sue@warrentopfarm.com
www.warrentopfarm.com

Sue Reynolds

Sommerhus at Warrentop Farm is a cottage B&B located five miles from Warrenton and seven miles from Round Top. The cottage has three bedrooms, two baths, a fully equipped kitchen, WiFi, TV and a stereo. Breakfast is provided upon request. The back deck overlooks a lovely pond, and a wood grill is available.

The cottage is perfect for girlfriend weekends and fishing groups. It is roomy and private. Fayette County Lake, with great bass fishing, and antiques stores are close by.

Q: *Do you offer any special services?*

A: Classes can be arranged for groups in crafts and cooking. Occasionally crafts and T-shirts are available for sale from my business, Schlosser by Design.

Texas Ranch Life

т. 979.865.3649
с. 979.885.8338
tauniae@aol.com
www.texasranchlife.com
John & Taunia Elick

10848 Cactus Lane
P.O. Box 803
Bellville, Texas 77418

Silver Saddle Smokehouse
310 Main Street
Bellville, Texas 77418

exas Ranch Life is an 1,800-acre guest ranch with eight authentically restored, luxuriously appointed guest homes. It offers the true Texas ranch experience, from open-range horseback riding and longhorn cattle drives to hunting, trophy bass fishing and even organic gardening. A restored 1910 chapel on the ranch hosts weddings. The barn has meeting space for corporate retreats and a large reception area. The covered arena hosts cutting and roping events and rodeos.

Q&A

Q: *Do you offer any special services or amenities?*

A: We offer free WiFi to guests, and spa services are available upon request. For the health-conscious guest, Texas Ranch Beef is naturally grown on the ranch and grass-fed with no hormones or antibiotics, and is available for purchase by the pound and also served at the Silver Saddle Smokehouse.

Q: *What inspired you to start your business?*

A: The desire to share with others the rural way of life that we have enjoyed for 32 years of marriage, and also to enable "city folks" to renew, refresh and strengthen their lives, marriages and family ties.

Q: *What's your favorite part of the "Round Top Experience"?*

A: How many of my guests during each Antiques Week often know each other or are neighbors and end up unknowingly staying on my ranch together. Happens every time …

RESTORED HISTORIC TEXAS HOMES

Featured in 2009 in *The New York Times* Home section, Texas Ranch Life guests can "bunk up" in eight authentically restored and luxuriously appointed historic Texas homes that were saved from demolition and moved to the ranch from nearby locations. Homes are furnished with antiques and heirloom pieces, heirloom pieces and oriental rugs, and feature modern conveniences plus luxury bedding, towels and robes.

RANCH LIFE AT ITS FINEST

The cowboy lifestyle is an American dream. At Texas Ranch Life guests enjoy open-range horseback riding on 1,800 acres featuring hills, trees and lakes — along with hundreds of Texas Longhorn cattle, American bison and other wildlife. Thirteen lakes offer great bass fishing, plus limited hunting packages are available for deer, dove/quail, or coyote.

Texas Ranch Life

DESTINATION RANCH WEDDINGS

With a restored 1910 chapel that seats up to 120, and one of the most scenic hilltops surrounded by 300-year-old live oaks and views of over 20 miles, Texas Ranch Life is a perfect wedding location. Guest homes sleep up to 60 people onsite and the climate-controlled horse barn has hosted receptions with more than 200 people. The Silver Saddle Smokehouse in nearby Bellville, which serves Texas Ranch Life ranch-raised longhorn beef, can provide catering, and outside caterers are also allowed.

CORPORATE RETREATS, MEETINGS, REUNIONS

Nestled off the beaten path, this country getaway is a perfect location for corporate groups and meetings. Guests bond over ranch activities such as branding, roping, shooting, tomahawk throwing, cattle drives, team penning, mechanical bull-riding and rodeos. Wireless Internet, satellite TV, projection equipment and home-cooked meals have made for great meetings for major oil companies, banks, and other large businesses from Texas and around the world.

Wellspring Retreat and B&B

580 Washington Street
P.O. Box 210
Round Top, Texas 78954
т. 979.249.2019
c. 832.646.1898
ljb@cvctx.com
www.wellspringretreat.net
Bob & Linda Brunson, *Owners*

$\mathscr{A}$ "wellspring" is "a place of abundant supply." A serene setting, relaxing quiet and great food are lavished on our guests. They love our attention to detail as well as the broad sweep of charm from the lush gardens and well-appointed rooms. Even the stars at night are a thrill!

Q: *Do you offer any special services?*

A: Wellspring is a perfect setting for weddings and special events. We have expertise in food, flowers and planning and provide one-stop coordination of memorable events. We go to great length to accommodate special requests, and guests love our breakfast buffet. I am known for my eggs!

Q: *What's your favorite part of the "Round Top Experience"?*

A: Having moved from the "big city," I have really enjoyed the generosity and helpfulness of my neighbors, and values that remind me of a time long past.

Q: *What inspired you to start your business?*

A: We thoroughly enjoy demonstrating hospitality and making the effort to be sure our guests get more than they expected. I also love living in such pleasant surroundings in charming Round Top!

Mushroom & Ham Savory Bread Pudding

Courtesy of the Outpost @ Cedar Creek Inn Kitchen

8 oz mushrooms

5 green onions, including green part, chopped

2 tsp garlic salt

Pepper, to taste

Seasoning salt, to taste

1 c chopped fresh ham

1 stick unsalted butter

Cubed bread in about 1-inch squares (can use old bread or rolls)

8 eggs

2 c milk

6 oz shredded Swiss cheese

- Preheat oven to 325 degrees.
- Cube enough bread to cover the bottom of a 9"x12" casserole pan.
- Sprinkle the bread with a little seasoning salt. Toast lightly in the oven for a few minutes, remove.
- Melt the stick of butter in a skillet and sauté the mushrooms with the garlic salt and pepper to taste until tender.
- Remove mushrooms from skillet with a slotted spoon, leaving the juices in the skillet.
- Return pan to stove and sauté the green onions and chopped ham just until tender.
- Mix with the mushrooms.
- Spread mixture and pour juices over the toasted bread cubes.
- In a bowl, beat the eggs with the milk.
- Pour over the prepared casserole.
- Sprinkle the shredded Swiss cheese over the casserole.
- Bake at 325 degrees for about 40 minutes or until cooked through and brown and bubbly on top.

SERVES 12

SERVICES

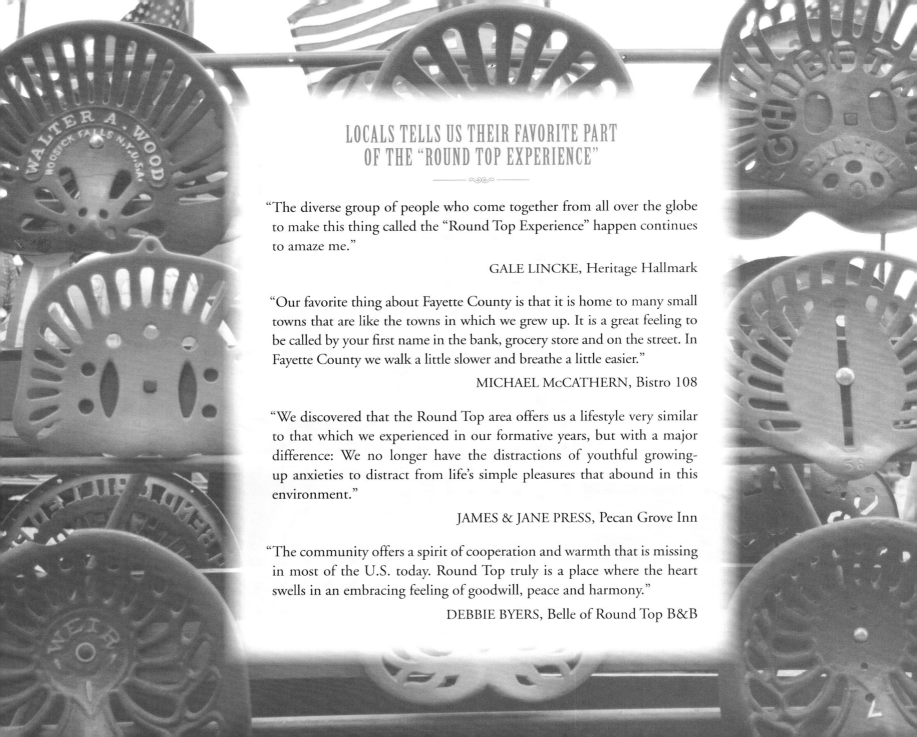

LOCALS TELLS US THEIR FAVORITE PART
OF THE "ROUND TOP EXPERIENCE"

"The diverse group of people who come together from all over the globe to make this thing called the "Round Top Experience" happen continues to amaze me."

GALE LINCKE, Heritage Hallmark

"Our favorite thing about Fayette County is that it is home to many small towns that are like the towns in which we grew up. It is a great feeling to be called by your first name in the bank, grocery store and on the street. In Fayette County we walk a little slower and breathe a little easier."

MICHAEL McCATHERN, Bistro 108

"We discovered that the Round Top area offers us a lifestyle very similar to that which we experienced in our formative years, but with a major difference: We no longer have the distractions of youthful growing-up anxieties to distract from life's simple pleasures that abound in this environment."

JAMES & JANE PRESS, Pecan Grove Inn

"The community offers a spirit of cooperation and warmth that is missing in most of the U.S. today. Round Top truly is a place where the heart swells in an embracing feeling of goodwill, peace and harmony."

DEBBIE BYERS, Belle of Round Top B&B

Deborah Bradley Events & Designs

Deborah Bradley

*D*eborah Bradley has more than 25 years' experience designing and coordinating events. With her vast background in interior decorating, graphic design and marketing, Deborah's talents allow her to consistently bring her clients' vision to light. With a select list of preferred vendors and professional staff, Deborah will plan, decorate and coordinate your entire event, from start to finish! "It's peace of mind ... by design."

La Grange, Texas
T. 1.800.886.6119
C. 979.702.1933
deborah@gottairon.com
www.deborahbradleyevents.com

Diane Mueller Photography

т. 979.733.3092
c. 979.725.8812   dianek@txun.net
La Grange, Texas   www.dianemuellerphoto.com

*D*iane Mueller is a portrait photographer working indoors as well as outdoors. "While I enjoy photographing inside my camera room, I also *love* going outside and on location to find the beautiful lighting and gorgeous scenery that surrounds me in the La Grange area. I specialize in high school seniors, children, families and weddings. Patients and flexibility are my greatest virtues," she said.

Diane Mueller

Q: *What is your area of expertise?*

A: I like to believe that I am known for the amount of time and attention that I give to my clients. People have often commented on my incredible patience in working in hectic situations.

Q: *Do you offer any special services?*

A: I offer custom-designed greeting cards, save-the-date cards, graduation announcements, and thank you notes.

Q: *Have you received any press recognition?*

A: My images were published in the *Eyes of Texas* calendar. I've also had images published in *Austin Weddings* magazine as well as *The Weimar Mercury* and *The Fayette County Record.*

Frank Hillbolt Productions

т. 979.249.6402
т. 979.249.5732
landandbass@gmail.com

301 North Live Oak Street
Round Top, Texas 78954

*F*rank Hillbolt Productions specializes in sound entertainment, providing *anything* involving sound for *any* occasion. From full band performances of various genres to canned music or a mic, from birthdays to weddings to auctions or fundraisers, I have done it all! From barns to boats, halls to the Hyatt, to the hills of west Texas, over 32 years of great times!

Frank Hillbolt

— Q&A —

Q: *Do you offer any special services?*

A: Live bands, DJs, musician referrals. Sound systems for rent. Guitar, amp and PA systems for rent. Anything to do with sound!

Q: *What inspired you to start your business?*

A: Jimi Hendrix … and the belief I can make *any* function or gathering a more festive experience!

Q: *What's your favorite Round Top story?*

A: I remember parking my BB gun under the giant oak tree in front of Scotty's because, back in the '60s, I was told I could not bring my gun into town!

Round Top Christian Fellowship

Matthew Diehl, *Pastor*
Jacob Sealy, *Full-time Youth Pastor*

Services:

Sunday Morning
Bible Study 9:00

Sunday Morning
Worship Service 10:30

440 East Mill Street
Round Top, Texas 78954
T. 979.249.5085
C. 979.661.8561
rtchurch@cvctx.com

SIMPLIFY. RENEW. GROW.

We are an interdenominational church, established in 1997, providing ministries for residents and visitors in the highly traveled Round Top community. Our mission statement is: "We exist to serve God by developing members to Christ-like maturity through love for God and man, as well as to prepare them for a ministry of service within the Church and local community."

-Q&A-

Q: *Do you offer additional services or activities?*

A: We offer an after-school mentoring program Monday through Friday and also host conferences and seminars.

Q: *What is your favorite part of the "Round Top Experience"?*

A: The opportunity to serve a diverse community.

Round Top Home Builders

Barney Reynolds

*R*ound Top Home Builders can build a custom home to your specifications from start to finish in as little as four months. We specialize in building Texas-style country homes from vintage woods and new materials and commit to only a few projects each year, ensuring the attention to detail you and your new home deserve. With more than 35 years of residential home-building experience, we provide top-quality construction, at a very competitive price along with integrity and dependability.

103 Main Street
Round Top, Texas 78954
т. 979.249.5151
с. 512.940.1299
barney1299@gmail.com
www.roundtophomebuilders.com

Round Top Real Estate

т. 979.249.5732
т. 877.249.5732
rtre@cvctx.com
www.roundtoprealestate.com

101 Main Street
P.O. Box 222
Round Top, Texas 78954

ound Top Real Estate has been in business for more than 20 years, assisting people with their real estate needs. Our expertise and experience have made real estate transactions an enjoyable event while making many friends along the way. We are best known for our knowledge of rural properties and matching that knowledge with potential buyers' needs.

Grover & Charlotte Hillbolt, *Brokers/Owners*

-Q&A-

Q: *Do you offer any special services?*

A: What sets us apart as a company is our knowledge of the area and the rural real estate market. As we work with clients, we love to introduce them to the area, invite them to local events, take them to concerts or plays and simply become friends. All of us are active volunteers and leaders in the everyday life of our community.

Q: *What's your favorite part of the "Round Top Experience"?*

A: We are constantly amazed by the publicity Round Top receives — the semi-annual Antiques Show, Royers Cafe, the 4th of July Parade, Festival Hill concerts with conductors from all over the world, the Chili Cook-Off…. We have it, plus the solitude of living in the country with cows, coyote and deer.

Round Top Real Estate:
Lilla Blackburn

ABR, Realtor®
101 Main Street
Round Top, Texas 78954
T. 713.301.3012
T. 979.249.5732
lillablackburn@gmail.com

I have been in real estate for the past 14 years. I started my career in Houston with Martha Turner Properties, where I learned how to be a top realtor and exhibit honesty, integrity and enthusiasm. Growing up, my family always had a weekend farm where we spent a lot of time, so I bought property here 10 years ago to fulfill my dreams. I love "showing off" Round Top, promoting the town and introducing people to life in the country!

Q&A

Q: *What is your area of expertise?*

A: Market knowledge is one of the most important requirements of real estate. I take the time to educate all of my clients about the market and make their needs and real estate goals my priority.

Q: *Do you offer any special services?*

A: When showing in Round Top, I like to give the "Round Top Tour" of what makes Round Top such a special place to be … including the library, Festival Hill, Winedale, the art galleries and restaurants.

Round Top Real Estate:
JoAnn Moss-Ayres

Broker Associate
101 Main Street
Round Top, Texas 78954
т. 979.249.5732
с. 979.249.7494
realtorjoannmossayres@gmail.com
www.joannmossayres.com

Since 1978, I have been engaged in real estate from many angles: commercial, residential, farm and ranch, and land development. As a multi-million dollar producer for several years, I have known the joy of matching buyers to new properties and the bittersweet experience of helping sellers turn over the family farm to new owners. We live in a beautiful place with wonderful people.

Q: *What is your area of expertise?*

A: Mostly selling country home sites. I have sold several ranches to developers and then sold the smaller farms created from them.

Q: *Do you offer any special services?*

A: Free market analyses of properties, multi-county searches for the right property, lots of information about the area, even listing property in France.

Round Top Real Estate:
Renee Diehl

Broker Associate
101 Main Street
Round Top, Texas 78954
т. 713.401.8958
realtor.diehl@gmail.com
www.roundtoprealestate.com

As a top-producing Realtor®, I assist buyers and sellers in the sale of rural property. My first job is understanding the goals of my clients and then providing accurate and relevant information so individuals can make the best choices for themselves. Connecting buyers and property owners to lenders, appraisers, surveyors, inspectors, general contractors and other trades is key in meeting the needs of my clients.

Q: *What inspired you to start your business?*

A: I love my home in the country. I enjoy helping others make their dreams a reality; whether it is their first home or their weekend place, which is their favorite home.

Q: *What is your favorite part of the "Round Top Experience"?*

A: I enjoy riding my bicycle down quiet country roads in the morning. Never know what 'critters' besides the cows I'm going to run into!

Round Top Real Estate:
Diane Langley

Realtor®
101 Main Street
Round Top, Texas 78954
c. 979.525.1324
dianelangleyrt@gmail.com
www.roundtoprealestate.com

*M*aking folks' dreams come true is my goal, whether they are looking for a farm or ranch or a place in one of our charming small towns for weekend or full-time living. You can kick back and relax or participate in the many and varied activities that go on throughout the year, from antiques to concerts to plays. This is the place!

Q: *What is your area of expertise?*
A: Selling mostly farms and ranches, but I also sell homes in Round Top, Carmine, Burton, Fayetteville and other towns and communities.

Q: *What inspired you to start your business?*
A: I'd love everyone to know the contentment of country living, even if only for the weekend.

Q: *What do you think attracts people to Round Top?*
A: The friendly atmosphere and the varied things there are to do in the area. You can soak up nature or culture all in the same place.

Round Top Real Estate:
Shelby Levy

Realtor®
101 Main Street
Round Top, Texas 78954
t. 979.249.5732
c. 713.857.9939
shelbyle@gmail.com
www.roundtoprealestate.com

I focus on helping people through the process of buying and selling property with the least amount of hassle. It is important to me to make the transaction as smooth and enjoyable as possible. After working in real estate for the past 25 years and working mostly with referrals from other clients, I am willing to listen to client needs and explore all the options.

Q: *What is your area of expertise?*
A: I bring a vast background of varied experiences, having worked as an elementary school teacher, civic and public school volunteer, master gardener, and volunteer docent at Bayou Bend in Houston and Festival Hill in Round Top. I have completed several continuing education courses, such as GRI (Graduate of the Real Estate Institute), CRS (Certified Residential Specialist) and ABR (Accredited Buyer Representative).

Round Top Real Estate:
Lisa Mayer

Broker Associate
101 Main Street
Round Top, Texas 78954
T. 979.966.3686
lmayer86@gmail.com
www.roundtoprealestate.com

*A*s a Broker Associate with Round Top Real Estate since 1996 and a realtor since 1986, Lisa provides a variety of real estate services and has been named top producer for her achievements. Customer service and building lasting relationships are Lisa's primary goals.

Q: *What is your area of expertise?*

A: Rural properties are Lisa's specialty. Her childhood ranching experiences and life on a Fayette County farm since 1982 provide her with a plethora of rural expertise. Lisa is also involved in many community activities, such as Lion's Club, 4-H Club, RT-C ISD District Advisory Board, Carmine Economic Development Board, and a Director of the South Central Board of Realtors.

Q: *Do you offer any special services?*

A: Lisa offers consultations for maintenance and improvements of country properties.

Round Top Real Estate:
Carole Nagel

Realtor®
101 Main Street
Round Top, Texas 78954
T. 970.249.5732
c. 979.966.2667
cnagel@cvctx.com
www.roundtoprealestate.com

I am a real estate agent for Round Top Real Estate. We list properties in Round Top and the surrounding area. I specialize in finding just the right property for my clients. Our staff takes pride in the service we offer our clients. We are open seven days a week.

Q: *What is your favorite part of the "Round Top Experience"?*

A: My favorite thing was being the first and only mayor of this special town. I love to go and tell everyone about all that Round Top has to offer. It's a little bit of heaven on earth.

Q: *What inspired you to start your business?*

A: When my husband passed away, I decided to go to Real Estate School. I was the oldest in my class and I had a great time. I passed!

Q: *Have you received any press coverage?*

A: I have been in the *New York Times* and other local media for my participation in the *Women of Round Top* calendar. Call me Miss July!

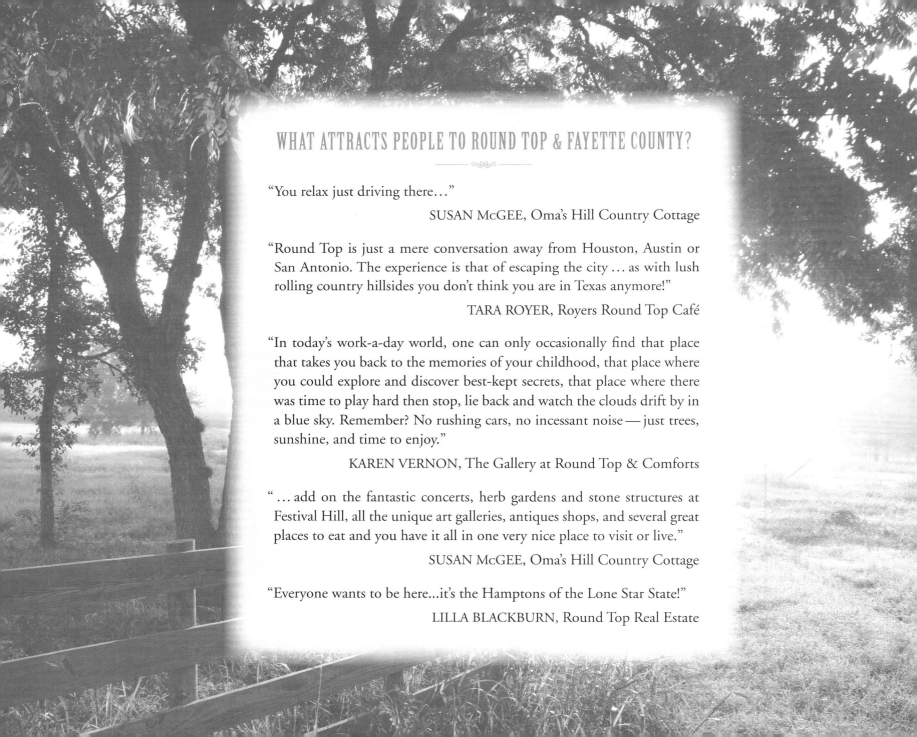

WHAT ATTRACTS PEOPLE TO ROUND TOP & FAYETTE COUNTY?

"You relax just driving there…"

SUSAN McGEE, Oma's Hill Country Cottage

"Round Top is just a mere conversation away from Houston, Austin or San Antonio. The experience is that of escaping the city … as with lush rolling country hillsides you don't think you are in Texas anymore!"

TARA ROYER, Royers Round Top Café

"In today's work-a-day world, one can only occasionally find that place that takes you back to the memories of your childhood, that place where you could explore and discover best-kept secrets, that place where there was time to play hard then stop, lie back and watch the clouds drift by in a blue sky. Remember? No rushing cars, no incessant noise — just trees, sunshine, and time to enjoy."

KAREN VERNON, The Gallery at Round Top & Comforts

" … add on the fantastic concerts, herb gardens and stone structures at Festival Hill, all the unique art galleries, antiques shops, and several great places to eat and you have it all in one very nice place to visit or live."

SUSAN McGEE, Oma's Hill Country Cottage

"Everyone wants to be here…it's the Hamptons of the Lone Star State!"

LILLA BLACKBURN, Round Top Real Estate

*P*art of the strength of the real estate partnership known in the Round Top area as "Your Home Team" is the 30+ year friendship between partners Betty Melton, Peg Richardson and Sandy Reed. The three friends formed "Your Home Team," working with the leading real estate company serving a five-county area — Heritage Texas Country Properties. These three savvy real estate pros share mutual respect and a common professional philosophy. For your country real estate connection this team's experience and professionalism is, as the HTCP motto states, "simply better"… just as it has been for years.

Your Home Team

at Heritage Texas Country Properties

Sandy Reed, Peg Richardson & Betty Melton

Sandy T. 979.966.3052
Peg T. 979.249.7584
Betty T. 979.966.3088

110 Bauer Rummel
Round Top, Texas 78954
T. 979.249.5767
peg@cvctx.com
www.ilovethecountry.com

Q: *What is your area of expertise?*

A: We specialize in farm & ranch, country properties, and home staging. We are also known for our tips: "The 10 Things You *Need* to Know Before Buying Country Property" and "How to Prepare Your Home and Property for Sale."

Q: *What do you think attracts people to Round Top?*

A: So many things: the proximity to Houston, Austin, and San Antonio; the gentle rolling hills; the cultural experience of both the visual and performing arts; the famous Antiques Show; the charming vintage farmhouses; but especially the people.

Strawberry Scones

Courtesy of The Shelby

4 c plus 1 Tbsp all-purpose flour

2 Tbsp sugar, plus additional for sprinkling

2 Tbsp baking powder

2 tsp salt

¾ pound cold unsalted butter, diced

4 extra-large eggs, lightly beaten

1 c *(minus 2 Tbsp)* cold heavy cream

2 Tbsp dry sherry or brandy

¾ cup small-diced strawberries

1 egg beaten with 2 Tbsp water or milk, for egg wash

- Preheat the oven to 400 degrees.
- In the bowl of an electric mixer fitted with a paddle attachment, combine 4 c flour, 2 Tbsp sugar, baking powder, and salt.
- Blend in the cold butter at the lowest speed and mix until the butter is in pea-sized pieces.
- Combine the eggs, heavy cream and sherry or brandy, quickly adding them to the flour and butter mixture. Combine until just blended. Remember that when mixing the scones, work the dough as little as possible to keep them tender.
- Toss the strawberries with 1 tablespoon of flour, add them to the dough, and mix quickly. The dough may be a bit sticky.
- Dump the dough out onto a well-floured surface and be sure it is well-combined.
- Flour your hands and a rolling pin and roll the dough ¾-inch thick. You should see lumps of butter in the dough.
- Cut dough with a heart-shaped cookie cutter or cut into squares and then triangles.
- Place on a baking sheet lined with parchment paper or a Silpat baking mat.
- Brush the tops with egg wash. Sprinkle with sugar and bake for 20–25 minutes, until the outsides are crisp and the insides are fully baked.
- Serve with crème fraiche (or whipped cream) and strawberry jam, if desired.

MAKES 14–16 LARGE SCONES

SHOPPING

the busy b

Holly M. Bargas, *queen b*

2204 East State Highway 71
La Grange, Texas 78945
T. 979.249.5132
busybgifts@hotmail.com
www.thebusyb.com

The busy b is an ever-changing shoppers' paradise! We pride ourselves on outstanding customer service and a wide array of products. From Pandora Jewelry, to baby gifts, to home accents — we strive to keep a good mix of "everything." Our customers have become our friends that we laugh and cry with. I love it when people come in just because they want to feel happy!

We opened B @ home about four years ago with exclusively holiday merchandise. However, it has grown and expanded into a year-round boutique filled with home accents and gifts.

Q&A

Q: *What is your area of expertise?*

A: We are best known for our wide array of products. I search high and low to find items you just don't see everywhere — even my sales reps ask "Where did you find that?"

Q: *What special services do you offer?*

A: I am a home stylist — we decorate for holidays and everyday living. And, we host several big events a year — including our famous Pajama Party!

Q: *What inspired you to start your business?*

A: From a young age, I was very independent and knew I wanted something of my own. My parents are self-employed — it's just in my blood!

Cottage Gatherings

T. 979.966.0555
152 North Washington Street
La Grange, Texas 78945

Cottage Gatherings is a fun, funky boutique nestled in the heart of historic downtown La Grange. We have all the new trends in ladies' clothing, shoes, and accessories and offer free alterations. We've been in business for almost 10 years. Also visit our home furnishings store, Urban Nest.

Hayley O. Johnson

—Q&A—

Q: *What are you known for?*

A: Our goal is to have great customer service. We want the customer to have a wonderful shopping experience every time they walk in the door.

Q: *What inspired you to start your business?*

A: The opportunity to be creative! I love all the unique stuff we sell.

Q: *Do you offer any additional services?*

A: Free alterations.

The Garden Company

T. 979.743.4648
C. 979.561.6257
gardenco@verizon.net

217 Kessler Avenue
Highway 77 South
Schulenburg, Texas 78956
Jeff & Stevie Thompson, *Owners*

The Garden Company combines a retail garden center and gift shop with a full-service landscaping and irrigation design and maintenance service. Our business is housed in a 1934 ranch house with almost two acres of nursery in downtown Schulenburg.

Q&A

Q: *What do you specialize in?*

A: Our garden center features organic gardening supplies and products. Our gift shop offers several lines of high-quality candles, lotions and jewelry and is expanding to feature work by local artisans, including painters and woodworkers. Our landscaping service evaluates our clients' outdoor living needs to optimize the solution. We feature certified irrigation specialists and four full-time rock masons to provide flagstone walkways, outdoor firepits and fireplaces, water fountains and gardens, and outdoor lighting. In addition, we offer seasonal or weekly landscape maintenance options.

Q: *Do you offer any special services?*

A: We do event planning for about six weddings per year. Stevie is extremely creative and handles all our landscape and event design.

Heritage Hallmark

240 West Colorado Street
La Grange, Texas 78945
T. 979.968.8555
heritage@cvctx.com

Gale Lincke

—Q&A—

Q: *What's do you think attracts people to the Round Top region?*

A: With the beautiful natural setting of this historic county, it's easy to understand why people love to come to the events every year. For those of us who have lived here all our lives, we think it's heaven and wouldn't trade our place for any other.

Heritage Hallmark, on the historic square in La Grange, brings together the best of Hallmark Cards and a family-owned hometown gift store. In this Gold Crown store, you'll find an incredible assortment of ways to express yourself, all personally chosen by Gale. From just the right card to the perfect gift, everyday occasions and seasons come alive in this bright, friendly store.

Le Petite Gourmet Shoppe

134 North Washington Street
La Grange, Texas 78945
T. 979.968.4000
lepetite@cvctx.com
www.lepetitegourmetshoppe.com

Not only is Le Petite a great place to shop for aspiring cooks, it's also the ideal place to find gifts for the person who enjoys cooking. You'll find an enormous selection of products including gadgets, cutlery, gourmet ingredients and all the kitchen essentials. Custom gift baskets and gift-wrapping services are also available.

Donella Dopslauf-Cernosek

Q: *What special services do you offer?*

A: We offer cooking classes, a gift registry service, and we make fabulous gift baskets.

Leftovers Antiques

Home | Mercantile

т. 979.830.8496
c. 979.421.2212
leftovers@texasbb.com
www.leftoversantiques.net

3900 Highway 290 West
P.O. Box 291
Brenham, Texas 77834
Ed Fulkerson & Michael Breddin, *Owners*

Gracie

Leftovers is a beautiful 10,000-square-foot home store featuring antiques obtained from all over the United States and Europe; an Apothecary with an abundant selection of soaps, lotions, and candles; a Mercantile with a huge variety of quilts, duvets, shams, throws, and pillows; and many other unique items for the home.

—Q&A—

Q: *What events do you host during the year?*

A: We host special events during Round Top Antiques Week, a Christmas Party and a Customer Appreciation event once a year.

Q: *Have you received any press recognition?*

A: Leftovers has been featured in publications including *Country Home, Cottage Style, Maine Antique Digest, LIVE Magazine,* and *Antiques Weekly.*

Q: *What inspired you to start your business?*

A: A love for the "retail business" and the "thrill of the hunt" when finding one-of-a-kind items.

Q: *What should everyone do while in Round Top?*

A: Enjoy the view and "shop till you drop"!

APOTHECARY

Leftovers has a lot to offer when it comes to soaps, lotions, and potions. Wouldn't a nice soak in a warm tub with soothing bath salts be the perfect ending to a long day? Or wake up to the fresh fragrance of a wonderful French milled soap! Who can resist a great lotion for hands or body? The selection is superb. Whether it's for self-pampering or a gift for a special friend, the selection at Leftovers has what you are looking for.

ANTIQUES

Leftovers strives for the unusual—the one-of-a-kind things that make a home yours. Through travels across America and Europe looking for unique furnishings and accessories, we allow you to express yourself and add the finishing touches to your home. We have formal and relaxed styles that allow for an assortment of looks that mix well together.

Leftovers Antiques

BEDDING

Snuggle under the covers with a good book and relax! That's the idea when it comes to the bedding at Leftovers. Soft and plush bedding makes everyone feel good. Styles and colors are personal, but with the large selection, your perfect mix can be achieved. Add a couple of pillows to change the mix of your existing bedding or select a new dust ruffle for a fresh feeling. Let us add the comforts to your bed.

THINGS GRANDMA DIDN'T HAVE

Antiques are the basis of Leftovers, but there are always things that add to a home that just didn't exist in Grandma's day. Every one loves a great book, and Leftovers offers a large selection of titles, from cooking to decorating. Grandmother's pearls are still a classic, but Leftovers' offering of sterling silver jewelry is a great way to pamper yourself. And though sofas were around in Grandma's day, they were hard. Today's designs allow us to offer a great selection of new sofas that offer modern comfort with the yesterday's style.

LizIz

т. 409.466.3228
lizizrt@yahoo.com

107 Main Street
Round Top, Texas 78954

izIz is Elizabeth Supple. She can be found most weekends at her store in downtown Round Top, LizzieLou's, pictured here. Her specialty is interior design work. For 20 years Elizabeth has been making beautiful homes — from beach resorts to ranches and farms — throughout Texas. LizIz is also known for her wedding creations, which include floral arrangements, tablescapes extraordinaire and parties of all kinds and sizes. Consultations and stagings are also welcomed.

Elizabeth Supple

Q: *What are you known for?*

A: Making ordinary into extraordinary. Just come by my shop LizzieLou's and see for yourself. Whimsy taken to a new level! You name it, Elizabeth Supple has done it in a fresh, new way.

Q: *What inspired you to start your business?*

A: My aunt, a noted artist. She always decorated for family functions and to this day I cherish those memories. I've been doing it for 20 years — I was a child prodigy!

Rhinestone Angel *and* The Flower Company

Kim Pape & Kaywin Pape Kubesch

501 I-10 Frontage Road, Exit 661
Flatonia, Texas 78941
T. 361.865.9026
T. 866.264.3545
rhinestoneangel@hotmail.com
www.rhinestoneangel.com
www.rhinestoneangel.blogspot.com

Rhinestone Angel and The Flower Company are owned and operated by a mother-daughter team, Kim Pape and Kaywin Pape Kubesch. Both have been florists for 12 years and specialize in wedding and event flowers. In 2003 the team opened Rhinestone Angel, which offers a unique mix of gifts, jewelry and home decor. From Pandora Jewelry to iron stars, Rhinestone Angel has something for everyone.

Q: *What are you known for at Rhinestone Angel?*

A: A great mix of gifts and home decor — Pandora Jewelry, Tyler candles, wrought iron decor, and eclectic home accessories.

Q: *Do you offer any special services?*

A: Rhinestone Angel offers holiday home decorating services.

Our mother-daughter team is always happy to meet new customers, help you find that special gift for a loved one, decorate your new table for the holidays, and work with any bride and groom to make their special day a dream come true.

Q&A

Q: *What is The Flower Company's area of expertise?*

A: We are known for creative floral designs, variety of decor elements, and attention to detail. In 2007 we were featured in *Florists' Review* for "Best Floral Cake Décor."

Q: *Do you offer any special services?*

A: The Flower Company has many rental items for weddings and events — iron candelabras, crystal chandeliers, cake plateaus and a large inventory of glassware.

Round Top Natural Soap

We manufacture and sell all-natural handmade soaps, lotions, creams and other skin care products. Our soaps are made with only botanical oils using the cold process method. We blend our own fragrances to give our products their unique scents. We are committed to caring for our earth, so we only use natural, renewable and sustainable soy wax and beeswax for all of our candles.

Jann Schwarz

Q: *What is your area of expertise?*

A: I formulate all of our products and fragrances, which we manufacture from scratch in our shop using the finest ingredients available. We recycle household items as containers and use containers made from recycled glass or that are reusable.

Q: *What inspired you to start your business?*

A: I love to create. I began making soaps for my family and friends. Then a local shop asked to sell my soaps. Slowly we built up a loyal customer base.

Q: *Have you received any press recognition?*

A: We have been covered in *Country Home*, *The Dallas Morning News*, *The Houston Chronicle*, *The Fayette County Reporter* and *The Show Daily*.

Schmidt Jewelry

т. 979.968.5149
jschmidt78945@verizon.net

118 North Washington Street
La Grange, Texas 78945

The Schmidt Jewelry store and gallery in La Grange is filled with Richard Schmidt's fabulous one-of-a kind pieces. You can also find work by other artists and unique gifts. The atmosphere is warm, the people are friendly and there's always a cold one the fridge.

Janet & Richard Schmidt

Q&A

Q: *What is your area of expertise?*

A: Richard is best known for his beautiful handcrafted jewelry. He mixes rugged turquoise with the brilliance of gemstones, sterling silver and yellow gold to create his jewelry. Christianity and its history have a large influence on his designs. Richard's work has been featured in *Cowboys and Indians, Cactus Creek Daily online, The Show Daily,* and *Women Out West.*

Q: *What inspired you to start your business?*

A: Richard is a fourth-generation Texan. He has been designing jewelry for almost a decade and is inspired by the great Southwest and Mexican folk art, having collected pottery, kachinas and retablos since the 1970's. Richard keeps his roots in La Grange, Texas, but loves the Southwest and spends as much time as possible in Santa Fe and southern Colorado. He loves what he does and will tell you that he is very fortunate and blessed to be able to create jewelry as a full-time job. "Jewelry with soul" is the best way to describe his work.

Sgovio

204 East Mill Street
Round Top, Texas 78954
T. 979.249.3618
info@sgovioboutique.com
www.sgovioboutique.com
Laura Sgovio, *Owner*

Offering an intoxicating experience of rural luxury, Sgovio Boutique is the creation of jewelry designer Laura Sgovio who in 1997, inspired by Round Top's beauty, found her passion for working with her hands. The 1880's building with stone walls and wooden floors blossoms with jewelry by six Texas designers, plus unique clothing, accessories and luxurious body care products.

Q&A

Q: *What's you area of expertise?*

A: We are "Where Women Discover Their Hidden Beauty." We specialize in unique and handmade jewelry and our ability to capture the essence of a woman.

Stoney Creek Antiques

Stoney Creek Antiques, in business for 25 years, is located in the charming old circa 1918 Carmine Hardware Company building. The building is packed with wonderful antique finds, both elegant and primitive, from all over the USA, Canada, and England. Transferware, stoneware, Americana, pottery, musical instruments, old picture frames, furniture, toys and games are just a few of the many antiques in our shop.

125 Augsburg Street
Carmine, Texas 78932
T. 979.278.3977
stoneycreekantique@swbell.net
Karen & Bob Springer, *Owners*

Texas Trash and Treasures

т. 423.502.1374
www.ilovecarmine.com

Turquoise building on
Highway 290
Carmine, Texas 78932

$\mathscr{G}$et ready for a Wow! experience when you enter the turquoise building in Carmine. Self-taught "country bumpkins" Richard and Linda Hamilton have created funky and whimsical designs for you to carry off. And if that isn't enough, they have combed the country to find other artists you probably have never seen. They specialize in bending and welding metal, steel, wire and East Tennessee tobacco barn tin into unexpected shapes and unnecessary stuff. Come see them during Antiques Week in Warrenton, across from St. John's food booth.

Linda & Richard Hamilton

—Q&A—

Q: *What inspired you to open shop near Round Top?*

A: Twenty-five years of roaming nationwide to art, craft and flower shows was enough! And it was a great excuse to be with my grandkids.

Q: *What's your favorite part of the "Round Top Experience"?*

A: "Boogying" back to Texas, finding and buying an old saloon, painting it *turquoise* and connecting with the Carmine community!

Urban Nest

т. 979.966.0111
148 North Washington Street
La Grange, Texas 78945

Urban Nest, located on the square in historic downtown La Grange, offers great stuff for your home. We have antiques, gifts, candles, furniture and bed linens — specialize in unique designs for home and office. Let us feather your nest! Also visit our ladies' clothing and accessories boutique, Cottage Gatherings.

Hayley O. Johnson

Q&A

Q: *What inspired you to start your business?*

A: After 10 years at Cottage Gatherings, I wanted to fulfill my love for antiques and design, so I decided to open a second store focused on the home.

Q: *What special services do you provide?*

A: We also offer event planning.

Q: *What's the best thing about your business?*

A: All my antique finds.

WHAT ADVICE WOULD YOU GIVE TO SHOPPERS AT ROUND TOP?

"Bring a big truck, a big wallet and plan to spend twice as much time as expected."

DENISE & RICK PRATT, Around the Bend

"Go with the flow. Local establishments work hard to provide good service and a good value. Sometimes the wait is a bit longer than normal—you'll enjoy the experience more if you relax."

KATHY JOHNSTON, Sterling McCall Antiques Showcase & Event Center

"Take your time and rush from venue to venue…like going on a European trip with 15 countries in 12 days, it cannot be accomplished. You need to stop at booths that "speak to you" and spend quiet time exploring what they have to offer. Turn your cell phone off, you cannot shop and talk …"

LINDA & LUDMIL MARCOV, Willow Nest

"Bring carts, sunscreen, an umbrella, rain boots, bottled water and packaging for delicate items."

VICKIE DAVIS, Texas Rose Show

"Don't skip the last tent the last row!"

CURTIS ANN DAVIS, Arbor Antiques Services

"Don't make a list. If you see it and you love it, better buy it or it will be gone before you get back."

JUDY HILL, J. Hill Designs

"No matter what anyone tells you, on your first visit you will never bring enough money or allow enough time to see it all! After eight years we still haven't seen it all! Take in as much as you can, read through the *Show Daily*—it is invaluable. Enjoy the *whole* experience … the shopping, the food, the people and, of course, all the treasures! Oh, and be prepared for *any* weather! This is not a "pack light" situation … bring a big truck!"

SUNDIE & BRAD RUPPERT, Vintage Sculpture

"Don't be intimidated by the size of the show. You may want to go into training a couple of months ahead of time if you're like me and *have* to see everything."

LINDA THOMPSON, Artifax Antiques & Design

ANTIQUES SHOW

THE ROUND TOP ANTIQUES SHOW

The Round Top Antiques Show is not *actually* a single antiques show and it's not actually just in Round Top. For about two weeks each spring and fall, antiques dealers from around the globe come to set up their wares at approximately 60 different venues stretching from Carmine south toward La Grange, and from Round Top and Warrenton east to Shelby and Fayetteville!

Top-notch dealers bring everything from vintage sterling, English majolica, original oil paintings, period lighting, fine furniture, antique books, and fine European linens to Depression glass, primitives, decorative collectibles, country store items and unusual folk art. As Emma Lee Turney told us, "If you can't find [what] you are looking for [at Round Top], it probably wasn't made!"

All of these antiques also bring shoppers from around the globe! So bring your patience as you navigate the inevitable traffic. You'll want to drive slowly—blink and you could miss "the find" at one of the venues set up along the side of the road. Look for more show advice from our dealers and venue owners in the following pages.

In this section you'll learn about some of the established Antiques Show venues and meet some of the dealers you'll encounter. The tradition started in 1968, when Miss Emma Lee Turney held the first Round Top Antiques Show at Rifle Hall with a mere 22 exhibitors. Over the 40 years since, many new venues have been added, bringing thousands of dealers and ensuring that the show has something for everyone.

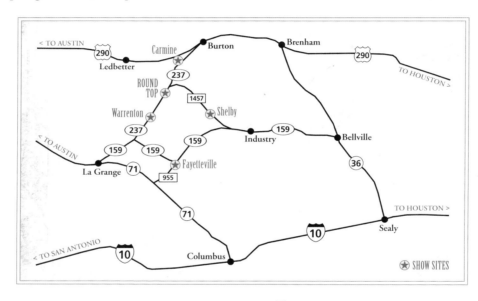

FEATURED VENUES INCLUDE:

- Arbor Antiques Services
- Blue Hills at Round Top
- CLUTTER
- EX•CESS
- Marburger Farm Antique Show
- The Original Round Top Antiques Fair
- Sterling McCall Antiques Showcase & Event Center
- Texas Rose Show
- Zapp Hall Antique Show

Events Schedule

The Round Top Antiques Show takes place twice a year, once in the spring and once in the fall (2010 dates are March 20 – April 4 and September 18 – October 2). The various venues operate independently and open and close on different dates within that window, with most shows open Wednesday through Saturday of the second week. Many venues also feature "shop late" nights on one or more evenings.

Some of the venues and dealers host events that have become show traditions, including:

° **Week 1 – Fri 4pm:**	Preview Party	CLUTTER
° **Week 2 – Tue eve:**	Wine & Cheese Party	Arbor Antiques
° **Week 2 – Tue eve:**	Preview Party	Rifle Hall
° **Week 2 – Wed eve:**	Grand Opening Party	The Big Red Barn
° **Week 2 – Thu eve:**	Junk Gypsy Junk-o-Rama Prom	Zapp Hall Antique Show

Also watch for an opening party at Leftovers in Brenham and Margarita Night & Wine Tastings at Pandora de Balthazar's air-conditioned tent at Arbor Antiques.

For information on upcoming Antiques Show dates and venues, visit the Round Top Area Chamber of Commerce website at www.roundtop.org or call them at 979.249.4042.

At the show, look for the *Show Daily* magazine for current venue, dealer and event information and a map to various show locations.

Junk Gypsy JuNK-O-RaMA Prom

Where: Zapp Hall Antique Show
When: Thursday night of the show in spring and fall

*W*hat started as a simple ode to the forgotten prom dress magically took a life of its own one night at the Round Top Antiques Show …

THE BEGINNING: During the show several years ago, we noticed the forgotten glory and beauty of a pile of vintage prom dresses and decided to pay tribute by hosting our own little JuNK-O-RaMA Prom. We scavenged the grounds, scooped up vintage dresses throughout the week and all played dress-up under the stars. There were a handful of customers and several "junkers" (aka vendors). We drank sangria, took silly pictures, practically danced holes in our boots, had lots of laughs … and were completely oblivious to the fact that JuNK-O-RaMA prom would soon become a legendary twice-yearly event.

TODAY: Nowadays, JuNK-O-RaMA Prom is much larger than a "handful of folks" — you probably couldn't stir 'em with a stick! It's a magical evening, complete with a rockin' band, a million and one twinkling Christmas lights, glittery chandeliers hanging out of the trees, and the absolute coolest "outhouse" in Texas.

The event has become a cultural crossroads of sights and sounds and people. And, we firmly believe, the happiest place on earth for one breathtaking evening in Texas. Under the big ol' southern stars you'll find a celebration for all ages and all walks of life, an evening where everyone truly is somebody!

The Arbor Antiques Services venue at Round Top is a 12-acre show featuring world-class antiques dealers from around the globe. Celebrating our 13th year in Spring 2010, Arbor Antiques has a solid reputation as a standout show and a "must-do" shopping destination while at Round Top. Look for our all-white tents one mile north of Round Top Square on Highway 237.

Consistent quality and variety are Arbor calling cards. Over the years we've become known for fine European and American antique furniture, antique linens, American primitives, and artist-signed Native American jewelry. We've got it all!

Curtis Ann & Dave Davis

Q & A

Q: *Where's the best place to eat during the show?*

A: Royers for dinner, of course, but there's this guy from Louisiana making *the best* catfish you'll ever put in your mouth. Each show brings someplace new. How do you find them? Funny... Everyone will be talking. It seems that eating in Round Top is second only to shopping!

Q: *What inspired you to start your business?*

A: Starting out as an exhibitor myself — renting space and having little or no voice over certain aspects of doing shows — made me want to implement my ideas and hopefully offer dealers and shoppers something more.

Q: *What's the most unusual thing you've ever sold?*

A: A letter written and signed by seven Indian chiefs to the president of the United States.

Q: *What advice would you give to the shoppers at Round Top?*

A: Don't skip the last tent in the last row!

The Parisian Cowboys

ROUND TOP ANTIQUES SHOW SERVICES

Shoppers are welcomed into our grounds with free parking and free admission. Hungry shoppers can eat a good breakfast or lunch in our cafe or try one of the food vendors on the grounds. Dealers and shoppers are able to check email or research their purchases with our WiFi service. Pitstops are easy and accessible in our clean and maintained air-conditioned comfort station or our handicapped facility. For those wanting to stay on-grounds for the evening, we have RV spaces with hookups.

SERVICES BEYOND
THE ROUND TOP ANTIQUES SHOW

Arbor Antiques Services operates estate sales in Texas and beyond and provides liquidation services to secure disposition of individual items or entire estates. We can market items on location, at combined sales, through Internet auctions and via our online site. We also provide competent and thorough appraisal services.

FOCUS ON THE ARTISTS

The Arbor Antiques Show at Round Top carries a large inventory of original artwork. You will have the opportunity to meet several renowned artists on-site as well as visit dealers carrying both antique and contemporary artwork.

Beautiful and quaint, Round Top has always been a Texas treasure to the 80 or so permanent residents. Through the vision of Miss Emma Lee Turney some 40 years ago this treasure is now opened for us all to enjoy. The Round Top Antiques Show is like a reunion. Season after season, year after year, dealers and shoppers alike come to the same place with their common interest — antiquing. Over the years, friendships develop and little traditions are celebrated. There's an atmosphere that has been nurtured, one that keeps us all coming back for more. It's not something you explain to someone, it's something you just have to experience Arbor Antiques is proud to be a part of the Round Top Show tradition and the Round Top Experience!

John Grafe Antiques & Interiors

ᵃ Arbor Antiques

T. 601.982.4344
C. 601.954.3984
jaximp@aol.com

622 Duling Avenue, Suite 205
Jackson, Mississippi 39216
John Grafe, *Owner*

We are a direct importer of Continental and English furnishings. We specialize in 18th and 19th Century painted furniture, gilt wood mirrors, unique chandeliers and lighting, dining tables and dining chairs, paintings, wrought iron consoles and garden items, tapestries, tortoise shell, Imari porcelain, porcupine quill, Majolica, Palissy ware, and many other decorative accessories.

-Q&A-

Q: What is your retail location like?

A: We are in a vintage remodeled elementary school built in the 1920's. It has 14' ceilings, long leaf pine floors, and exposed brick walls.

Q: What tip would you give to new collectors?

A: Try to buy something wonderful for yourself at least once a year and you will one day have a home full of treasured items!

Q: What inspired you to start your business?

A: My grandmother was a talented artist and painter and she passed on her love of beautiful things and a sense of creativity to me at a very early age.

Q: What is your favorite part of the "Round Top Experience"?

A: I have always enjoyed the people who come through the shows to shop. It never ceases to amaze me as to the overall knowledge of buyers. They are "seasoned" and obviously well-travelled, showing a superb eye toward — and the ability to purchase — both the decorative and quality antiques that are found in abundance at Round Top.

Pandora de Balthazar
European Luxury Bedding

ᵒ Arbor Antiques

T. 979.249.2070
C. 850.450.4634
info@pandoradebalthazar.com
www.pandoradebalthazar.com

201 East Austin Street
Round Top, Texas 78954

698 East Heinberg Street
Suites 102-104
Pensacola, Florida 32502

*R*arely has a shop displayed such an extensive collection of antique textiles in the midst of a field. Join Pandora de Balthazar as she brings the finest European luxury bedding, Hungarian goose down European sleep system, handmade lavender spa collection, and incredible antique textiles, pillows, tapestries, laces and fine linens for the bed and home. With more than 3 million pieces in her textile collection, Pandora de Balthazar and her knowledgeable staff present this exquisite collection of "paintings in thread."

Pandora de Balthazar

— Q&A —

Q: *What is your favorite thing to do during the show?*

A: Sleep! We're here for three weeks and our days are 12 to 16 hours long, so taking my shoes off and relaxing in front of the fireplace, having a glass of wine and then getting into my bed is manna from heaven.

Q: *What inspired you to start your business?*

A: I created the European sleep system after an injury and subsequent years of physical discomfort. Now my mission is to share my products and knowledge and to help others overcome sleep issues and create sleeping environments that enhance one's quality of life.

CUSTOMIZE YOUR SLEEP ENVIRONMENT

Take time to experience the difference with the European sleep system. Made from Hungarian goose down and feather, this collection of pillows, duvets, mattress pads, blankets, travel pillows and more will change your life. With the goal of increasing REM sleep, Pandora's team of experts will teach you how to enjoy pillows that "merge your body with the mattress." Enhance your bed with a down mattress pad, dress your bed to cool it down or warm it up … a comfortable body and mind makes for a better and longer night's sleep.

PAJAMA PARTIES AT THE BYBEE FARMHOUSE

What secrets can one find in tiny Round Top? Right behind the Mercantile, on Bybee Road, the infamous Faith Bybee's farmhouse has been brought to life by Pandora de Balthazar and her luxury bedding team. Timeless yet faithful to history, this museum home is richly appointed in true Round Top, Texas style with luxuriously comfortable linens, European sleep system and antique furnishings — all for you to enjoy. Contact us for guest house reservations and ask about our private pajama parties, the masseuse, or your very own private shopping experience in the historic Ima Hogg House on Bybee Square.

BYBEE FARMHOUSE
306 Bybee Road
Round Top, Texas 78954
T. 979.249.2070

RESTORATION, CUSTOMIZATION, RETROFITS & REPAIR

Collectors of antique textiles will be excited to meet Pandora and see her one-stop shop. Design your own headboard or have it monogrammed. Select your chairs and have them slip-covered. Try out your mattress and pick out the pillows and sheets. Have your windows custom-covered with lace or motorized Roman shades made of antique linen. Design custom-made table linens for your dining pleasure. We can also restore and repair your most treasured family heirlooms. Come see, touch and explore the beautiful possibilities of antique textiles in your own home.

Pandora de Balthazar

wendow fine living

ᵒArbor Antiques

т. 512.284.9732
т. 512.497.6294 *show week only*
info@wendowfineliving.com
www.wendowfineliving.com

1512 West 35th Street Cutoff
Suite 100
Austin, Texas 78731

𝒲endow Fine Living is Austin's premier home furnishings store, featuring an eclectic mix of 18th & 19th Century antiques combined with transitional, chic, and industrial finds. Our mission is to stay ahead of the trends, exceeding clients' expectations and cultivating long-term relationships. Wendow specializes in one-of-a-kind lighting, custom upholstery, and unique gifts and accessories.

Shannon Dowell & Catherine Wenske

-Q&A-

Q: *What do you specialize in?*

A: Wendow's emphasis is mostly on French antiques, though one might see an occasional nod to Italy or Spain. Mostly our look is transitional, combining antiques with new pieces, urban or industrial. We offer in-home consultations as well.

Q: *What inspired you to start your business?*

A: The need for a sophisticated design source/store in Austin.

Q: *What's your favorite part of the "Round Top Experience"?*

A: The thrill of the hunt and the excitement over a great find!

Antiques Show Venue

Blue Hills at Round Top

Highway 237
North of downtown Round Top

Loblolly General Goods

Blue Hills: *Pavillion A*

813 Main Street
Bastrop, Texas 78602
т. 512.308.1168
loblollygoods@att.net
www.pulleylight.blogspot.com

*L*oblolly offers quality American and European antique furnishings, antique lighting, local works of art and jewelry, folk art and unique gifts. For more than 15 years our line of residential pulley lights have been the mainstay of our business. Last year our pulley lights were featured in over 20 editorial pictorials in national interior design magazines such as *Architectural Digest, Country Living,* and *Better Homes and Gardens.*

Marc Elson

Q&A

Q: *What keeps you coming back to the Round Top Antiques Show?*

A: The beautiful setting of Round Top, Texas. My favorite thing to do during the show is visit Festival Hill. Everyone should visit the herb garden there while in Round Top.

Brocante

David & Martha Parnell

Blue Hills: *Barn A*

Lake Charles, Louisiana
T. 337.802.9645
T. 337.439.5836
brocante@suddenlink.net

ince 1999 we have been traveling the back roads of France in search of wonderful French country antiques and unusual decorative items with stories to tell. We personally select our merchandise and strive to offer an eclectic mixture of fine and interesting antiques that capture the French country style and experience.

We are often asked what "Brocante" means. In France, brocante shops are generally a mixture of period antiques plus "objects of charm" that represent the life and work of the people. It is this mixture that defines the Country French style.

Q&A

Q: *What is your area of expertise?*

A: In addition to 18th and 19th Century French country furniture, we specialize in French copper, pottery and unusual decorative and architectural pieces that represent the history and everyday life of the people in Southern France.

Q: *What's the most unusual thing you've ever sold?*

A: In the hayloft of a barn in Southern France we discovered more than 100 carved panels that had lined the walls of a chateau in that region.

Q: *What is the one thing everyone should do (besides shop!) while in Round Top?*

A: Get off the main roads and take some time to enjoy the beautiful scenery and history this region offers.

LOOK FOR BROCANTE IN THESE FINE LOCATIONS:
- The Foyer in Baton Rouge, Louisiana T. 225.343.3655
- Circa 1857 in Baton Rouge, Louisiana T. 225.387.8667
- Passages Antiques in New Orleans, Louisiana T. 504.899.3883
- Memorial Antiques & Interiors in Houston, Texas T. 713.827.8087

Antiques Show Venue

CLUTTER

Shirley & Staci Schwantz

3949 Highway 237
Warrenton, Texas
Next to EX•CESS

T. 979.249.3682 *show week only*
cluttershow.com

W̲e sell an eclectic mix of things we love: English transferware and old prints from the 1800's, painted furniture, industrial furniture, mechanical items, textiles and jewelry. We travel to England, Mexico and throughout the U.S. to find things that are unusual and interesting. We only sell them at this show twice yearly. We offer good discounts to dealers.

Come shop and stay for gourmet sandwiches at Sack Lunch at CLUTTER, located in the vintage Airstream trailer in the tent out back.

Sack Lunch

CLUTTER: *in the back*

3439 Highway 237
Round Top, Texas 78954
т. 512.417.4432
sharonbright@att.net
www.sharonbright.com

Sack Lunch is a mobile food site, serving out of a 1954 Airstream trailer. The type of food is based on casual picnic fare, classics revisited and the freshest-quality ingredients that I can find and use. The business is only set up at CLUTTER two times yearly. Catering is available all year round. I serve really fresh food that isn't fried or on a stick!

Sharon Bright

Q&A

Q: *What inspired you to start your business?*

A: I used to do set-up for CLUTTER. I would have to bring my own coffee and food. Life is way too short to eat yucky food. It seems to me that antiques dealers really respond to good, quality ingredients and tasty, classic comfort food.

The Coffee Bug

Brad Frank

Granny McCormick's Yard
Warrenton, Texas

Hesperus, Colorado
T. 800.579.8510
www.thecoffeebug.com

*L*ocated in Granny McCormick's Yard, across the road from the Warrenton Grocery & Old Feed, the Coffee Bug is a 1969 VW Beetle "coffeewagon." It's essentially a traveling coffeehouse, featuring a full menu of espresso drinks, fresh fruit smoothies and coffee slushies. Open at 6AM for early risers!

Antiques Show Venue

EX·CESS

3907 State Highway 237
Warrenton, Texas 78954

Flat Earth Designs

Oliver Whitman & Richard Taylor

EX•CESS

flatearthdesigns@bellsouth.net

Wholesale Inquiries Only

*R*ichard and Oliver specialize in concrete decorative accessories. Their business is almost exclusively wholesale and they sell to top design stores around the country. Their booth at EX•CESS during Antiques Week is their only retail location and offers customers a unique opportunity to see the breadth of their product line and to meet the designers in person.

KING + QUEEN
CROWNS
$ 10—

Pieces of the Past

Kathy Johnson

*P*ieces of the Past specializes in architectural antiques and antique reclaimed lumber. We always have vintage doors from across the USA and a great inventory of old Mexican doors, in addition to barnwood, pine flooring, and bead board. Many pieces are one-of-a-kind. We also carry beautiful furniture made from vintage wood, with and without finishes.

Q: *What keeps you coming back to the Round Top Antiques Show?*

A: This is a hard job, but it so rewarding because of the customers, many of whom have become very good friends. My life is richer than from any job where I made more money.

EX·CESS

104 Highway 281 South @
Highway 290 West
Johnson City, Texas
T. 512.784.8246
F. 830.868.2890
kj@kjtexas.com
www.pieces-of-the-past.com

Recycling the Past

Matthew White, *Finder of Objects*

EX•CESS

381 North Main Street
Barnegat, New Jersey 08005
T. 609.660.9790
T. 609.618.7606 *show week only*
recycling@comcast.net
www.recyclingthepast.com

*R*ecycling the Past is architectural salvage. We travel the globe dismantling old buildings and sourcing funky finds. Items are either turned into one-of-a-kind works of art — tables, furniture, etc. — or sold as-is in our yard. We have antique doors, mantles, tile, flooring, stone and industrial items, just to name a few, and more than 3,000 items can be found online!

Architectural salvage is our main focus — dismantling buildings before the wrecking ball comes. We are known for our high stone dismantling, and doing the crazy jobs no one else will do!

—Q&A—

Q: *What tip would you give to new collectors?*

A: Buy what you like. You gotta look at it if you don't!

Q: *What are you passionate about collecting?*

A: I'm really not a collector. I am a temporary storage facility until someone else likes it more!

Q: *What is your retail location like?*

A: It's been called "The Secret Garden Meets the Most Amazing Shop You've Ever Seen."

Q: *What keeps you coming back to the Round Top Antiques Show?*

A: The hope that someone will buy everything in one shot!

Unique Stone

Jason & Alex Perakis

EX•CESS
Texas Rose Show

1662 Highway 74 East
Hamlet, North Carolina 28345
T. 910.582.5445
T. 910.995.1950
uniquestone@carolina.rr.com
www.uniquestone.com

We are modern-day artisans of sculpture from times long past, using techniques like Faux Bois. We have also collected some of the finest antique garden statuary from all over the world and we reproduce these one-time originals so that they can be enjoyed in your present-day garden. We offer only the finest quality cast stone reproductions, which earn us our name, Unique Stone.

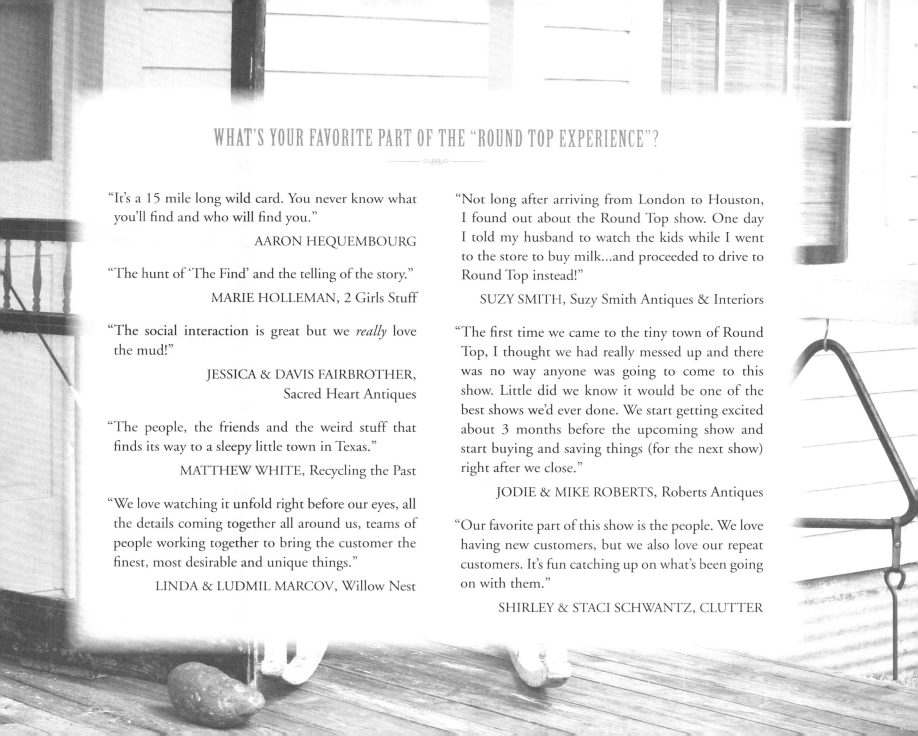

WHAT'S YOUR FAVORITE PART OF THE "ROUND TOP EXPERIENCE"?

"It's a 15 mile long wild card. You never know what you'll find and who will find you."

AARON HEQUEMBOURG

"The hunt of 'The Find' and the telling of the story."

MARIE HOLLEMAN, 2 Girls Stuff

"The social interaction is great but we *really* love the mud!"

JESSICA & DAVIS FAIRBROTHER,
Sacred Heart Antiques

"The people, the friends and the weird stuff that finds its way to a sleepy little town in Texas."

MATTHEW WHITE, Recycling the Past

"We love watching it unfold right before our eyes, all the details coming together all around us, teams of people working together to bring the customer the finest, most desirable and unique things."

LINDA & LUDMIL MARCOV, Willow Nest

"Not long after arriving from London to Houston, I found out about the Round Top show. One day I told my husband to watch the kids while I went to the store to buy milk...and proceeded to drive to Round Top instead!"

SUZY SMITH, Suzy Smith Antiques & Interiors

"The first time we came to the tiny town of Round Top, I thought we had really messed up and there was no way anyone was going to come to this show. Little did we know it would be one of the best shows we'd ever done. We start getting excited about 3 months before the upcoming show and start buying and saving things (for the next show) right after we close."

JODIE & MIKE ROBERTS, Roberts Antiques

"Our favorite part of this show is the people. We love having new customers, but we also love our repeat customers. It's fun catching up on what's been going on with them."

SHIRLEY & STACI SCHWANTZ, CLUTTER

Antiques Show Venue

Marburger Farm

T. 800.999.2148
T. 979.249.3260 *show week only*
rick@marburgershow.com
www.roundtop-marburger.com

2248 South Highway 237
Round Top, Texas 78954
Rick McConn &
Ashley Ferguson, *Owners*

_M_arburger Farm is an outdoor antiques show on 43 acres featuring more than 350 dealers from the U.S. and abroad. Dealers can be found in 10 large tents and 12 historic Texas buildings. Our show is held twice a year in the spring and fall. An extraordinary range of antiques is offered, including Americana, Continental, French, English, early Texas, industrial, painted furniture, silver, fine art and estate jewelry. Our venue is also available for private events.

SHOPPERS CAN EXPECT TO FIND:

- The best antiques at the best prices
- Incredible selection in all price ranges
- Never-before-seen antiques offered to the public
- A full-service show—from the cafe to the delivery company

Q&A

Q: What is your favorite part of the "Round Top Experience"?

A: Round Top has so much history! As a native Houstonian, it was significant to me that Houston women philanthropists identified Round Top as a place to promote and preserve. While at the show, be sure to explore the town, including the library and Festival Hill, and the beautiful bucolic countryside around it.

Q: What inspired you to start your business?

A: We were looking to find a family business and leave the corporate world behind. With a love of antiques and design, and a perfect location — in the foothills of the Texas Hill Country and close to both Houston and Austin — Marburger Farm was a great fit.

EXTENSIVE SHOW SERVICES

Over the years a full-service café, on-site shipping service, free WiFi, air-conditioned comfort stations and a shuttle service have been added to satisfy the growing demand from our dealers and shoppers. This commitment to dealers and shoppers is what makes Marburger Farm the ultimate antiques destination.

INTERNATIONALLY ACCLAIMED ANTIQUES SHOW

Marburger Farm Antique Show was started more than 12 years ago and has grown from one tent to 10 large tents showcasing more than 350 dealers over 43 acres. Our dealers are from nearby towns and other countries. The extraordinary range of antiques in all price ranges is what makes the show such a destination for shoppers, designers and dealers.

The Marburger Farm Antique Show is regarded by *Newsweek* and other media as one the best antiques shows in the country. The show is consistently covered by the "antiques world" press, from *Maine Antique Digest* to *Antiques and the Arts*. In addition to the antiques press, Marburger Farm has been profiled in such publications as *Arthur Frommer's Budget Travel, Texas Home & Living, Austin Monthly* and *Country Living*.

A HOME TO HISTORIC TEXAS BUILDINGS

There are 12 historic circa-1900 buildings on the Marburger Farm property. These early Texas buildings have been relocated from their original locations in Fayette County with the exception of the Saloon, which was relocated from Yorktown, Texas. Ranging from single-room homes to the original Marburger Farm House to a blacksmith shop to a dance hall to a general store and a bingo hall, these buildings house antiques dealers during our show and are available for events.

CELEBRATE YOUR SPECIAL EVENT AT MARBURGER FARM

Marburger Farm Events is a recent complement to our venue. With the historic buildings and beautiful pastureland as a backdrop, events such as weddings, receptions, rehearsal dinners, live music, reunions, birthday parties, graduation parties, photography sessions and picnics all happen here. Chic rural or elegant country rules as Marburger Farm can be transformed into your dream event destination. Marburger Farm can host outdoor ceremonies or indoor functions, intimate groups or large parties for any event.

Marburger Farm

2 Girls Stuff
° Marburger Farm: *Tent C*

т. 214.460.2523
c. 214.727.0404
hollemanantiques@tx.rr.com

Rhonda Holden & Marie Holleman

2 Girls Stuff is a collaboration of ideas and the creative talent of two friends who seek out unusual items — from found objects to the most extravagant treasures. We love to think outside the box with what we find and encourage others to do the same.

— Q&A —

Q: *What's the best advice about antiques you ever received?*

A: An antique does not have to be in perfect condition to be loved and appreciated.

Q: *What are you known for?*

A: Our "Industrial Cowboy" and one-of-a-kind items.

Q: *What advice would you give to the shoppers at Round Top?*

A: Great Stuff Doesn't Last. If you like it, you'd better buy it.

2 Lucy's

∘ Marburger Farm: *Tent A*

т. 713.304.0442
т. 713.825.0045

info@2lucys.com
www.2lucys.com

8719 Katy Freeway
Houston, Texas 77024

2 Lucy's, located in Houston, is an antiques business started by two friends in 2005. Kelly and Tracey (aka 2 Lucy's) travel to Europe several times a year looking for beautiful and unusual pieces to add to their inventory. Known for their eclectic style, the 2 Lucy's aren't afraid to mix things up. They carry anything from 17th Century French to more contemporary, industrial pieces.

Kelly O'Donnell & Tracey Shingledecker

2 Lucy's

Q&A

Q: *What is your area of expertise?*

A: Known for our unusual mix of antiques, we love a little bit of everything: traditional, rustic and contemporary pieces. We like to give new "life" to old items by finding unusual ways to use them.

Q: *What inspired you to start your business?*

A: In 2004 we began importing antiques from Europe for our own homes. After being encouraged by friends and family, we decided to start our own business. After six years we are still growing.

Q: *What is your favorite Round Top story?*

A: The first time we participated at the Marburger Farm show, the famed designer Charles Faudree came in with a client and bought a beautiful antique commode from us. Having read his books and admired his work, this was a thrill. Then a few hours later, Jennifer Jordan, the photographer who shoots Faudree's books, came in and asked if she could snap a few pictures of our space. We were pleasantly surprised to find a photo of one of our antique wooden horses featured in her latest book, *Horses & Homes*. A photo of that same horse was used for the Marburger ad in the October '09 issue of *Veranda*.

Specializing in French and continental antiques, the two travel the French and wider European countryside searching for beautiful furniture and accessories. Although they are especially fond of early French provincial pieces, their inventory includes antiques from all over Europe including Spain, Italy, Germany and Belgium, with items ranging from the 17th to the early 20th centuries. When people ask how they decide what to buy, the two have a very simple answer: "We only buy what we love."

Aaron Hequembourg

⁹ Marburger Farm: *Outside The Saloon*

т. 404.403.3541
info@bigwhitedog.net
www.bigwhitedog.net

522 Herds Creek Road
Monticello, Georgia 31064

For more than seven years Aaron Hequembourg has been producing paintings engraved into materials salvaged from sharecropper houses on the circa-1812 plantation where he lives with his wife, Hope, and their four children. Aaron researches period photography to inspire images that are engraved through vintage book text onto salvaged wood. The resulting work speaks to the appeal of old photographs and the history that he lives in.

Aaron Hequembourg

—Q&A—

Q: *What is your area of expertise?*

A: The images are inspired from actual photographs ranging from the 1880's to the 1930's. My favorite part is marrying them to the array of materials from the farm.

Q: *What inspired you to start your business?*

A: Aaron and his wife were married in the front yard of the historic farmhouse. The history and structures of the plantation inspire the work.

Antica Collection

We are direct importers of fine antiques and collectibles from all around Europe. We handpick each piece and spend eight months of the year on the "Old Continent" to look for treasures. We specialize in early 16th, 17th, and 18th century pieces from Italy, France and Spain, including furniture and devotional paintings and carvings.

Lisa Strait & Eric Vanpoucke

-Q&A-

Q: *What inspired you to start your business?*

A: The religious art in European and South American churches and museums.

Q: *What is your favorite thing to do during the show?*

A: Have fun with friends and clients, drink, and share good dinners.

Q: *What's the most unusual thing you've ever sold?*

A: An Italian chandelier that was nine feet tall and nine feet wide!

Antique Maps & Works on Paper

∘ Marburger Farm: *Tent F*
∘ Blue Hills: *Barn A*

T. 505.660.2688
info@antiquemapsandworksonpaper.com
www.antiquemapsandworksonpaper.com
Santa Fe, New Mexico

xperts in antique maps and art work on paper, "Parisian Cowboy" David Deighton and his wife, Natasha, offer thousands of original pieces spanning more than 500 years of history, to decorate your walls. Their maps and works on paper are featured in several museums and private collections in the U.S. and Europe.

Natasha & David Deighton

Q&A

Q: What inspired you to start your business?

A: David's French grandfather gave him his first antique map — it was of the USA! Now, 25 years later, David and Natasha are avid collectors of antique maps and art and love sharing their passion with others.

Q: What's your favorite part of the "Round Top Experience"?

A: Having a great time. I'm from France and Natasha is from England, where we were sheltered from the Texas mud, dust, bugs and heat, but Texas always treats us well. We love Texas and Texans love our collection of maps and antique works on paper. We always have a great Round Top Experience!

Around the Bend

◦ Marburger Farm: *Tent G, The Artisan Tent*

т. 330.345.9585
willow@sssnet.com

7883 Cleveland Road
Wooster, Ohio 44691

round the Bend offers a traditional and contemporary blend of unique, creative and colorful willow furnishings for your home and garden. We custom-build each order so we can make adjustments to sizes and colors.

Rick & Denise Pratt

-Q&A-

Q: *What inspired you to start your business?*

A: My wife inspired me to build furniture, but our business happened by a demand from people to make more!

Q: *What is your favorite part of the "Round Top Experience"?*

A: This is the most complete buying experience in the country! There is something for everyone. Bring a big truck, a big wallet, and plan to spend twice as much time as expected!

Artifax
antiques & design

Marburger Farm: *Tent A*

at Red Rooster Antique Co.
386 West San Antonio
New Braunfels, Texas 78130
T. 830.660.8759
www.artifaxantiques.com

Rex & Linda Thompson

G enerations, comfort, history, unique, authentic, creative. These are just a few words and feelings we try to express through a single object or an entire room. We are always on the hunt for those special items, and each piece must catch the eye with its visual story and history.

-Q&A-

Q: *What is your area of expertise?*

A: We specialize in antique/vintage painted furniture, artwork, paintings, photographs and prints. Our clients know they can find just what they didn't even know they needed.

Austin Woodhenge

We sell botanical pictures that are copied onto handmade paper and we paint the frames to look old. We also make small furniture, one-of-a-kind jewelry, dyed and printed "paperboy" bags, papier-mâché dress forms, and pillows made from antique linen grainsacks that we also use on our bags. We love to use antique and vintage things to make new things. We repurpose!

Kathy & Don Gross, *Artisans*

-Q&A-

Q: What's the most unusual thing you've ever sold?

A: A large convex mirror painted to look like a bloodshot eye!

Q: What inspired you to start your business?

A: Closing a retail fabric store and building movie sets, but mainly a three-week trip to London, the South of France, and northern Italy in 1998.

Marburger Farm: *Tent G,*
The Artisan Tent

11409 Highway 620 North
Austin, Texas 78726
T. 512.258.1393
C. 512.809.2991
kathyawh@sbcglobal.net
www.austinwoodhenge.com

D. Redington Design

Dakota R. Pratt

Marburger Farm: *Tent G,
The Artisan Tent*

428 23rd Street
Manhattan Beach, California 90266
т. 614.352.8200
dakotarpratt@gmail.com
www.dakotapratt.com

D. Redington Design offers contemporary, functional sculptures made of a wood base with flattened vintage bottle caps or a willow inlay design finished with a two-part epoxy resin. Each cap is flattened by hammer on a steel block, 8-12 hits per cap! Use of steel and antique bases also plays a role in my sculptures and furniture.

Q: *What inspired you to start your business?*

A: Growing up in my parents' workshop and going to art shows since I can remember.

Eclectic Architecturals

David & Sharon Cox

Marburger Farm: *Tent D*

1201 Champion Way
Longview, Texas 75604
т. 903.234.0016
c. 903.720.1381
info@earchitecturals.com
www.earchitecturals.com

*E*clectic Architecturals, located in a 10,000-square-foot-warehouse in Longview, Texas, offers a mix of antiques, reproduction pieces and modern art. Our specialty is doors from around the world. Doors and other items can be modified to meet customers' specific needs. As our name implies, we do not have a particular look, but an eclectic mix that suits many tastes and prices.

Q: *What's the most unusual thing you've ever sold?*

A: A polychrome antique door from a Catholic girls' school.

Elephant Walk Interiors & Antiques

Elephant Walk is central Florida's premiere gallery for high quality antique furniture, accessories and architectural elements. Specializing in European and Continental selections from around the world, Elephant Walk offers an extensive inventory of antiques to satisfy any design challenge. Our area of expertise would certainly be European country pieces, with their honest down-to-earth colors and textures. I love large-scale pieces, which seems to better suit today's interiors

Ender Tasci

Q: *What's the best advice about antiques you've ever received?*

A: Twenty-one years ago, when I first started in this business, an older antiques dealer was set up across from me at a show. He told me to "be very careful and only buy what you love, because you never get rich in this business, you only get rich *in inventory*." Which was very true. Today Elephant Walk occupies over 23,000 square feet of warehouse and showroom space!

Q: *What is your retail location like?*

A: It's crazy ... an overload of textures, layered with wonderful things that I am so passionate about!

Found Images

Marburger Farm: *Tent G,*
The Artisan Tent

824 Travis Street
Wichita Falls, Texas 76301
T. 800.295.7797
C. 940.867.1675
foundimages@sbcglobal.net
www.found-images.com
Catherine Miles & Jon Miles, *Owners*

For 22 years, we have used images we find to print on T-shirts, lampshades, pillows, and other gifts. Our retro images are from vintage postcards, fabric, and books and are hand-printed in Texas. My brother Jon makes lamp bases out of fallen trees and we also make lamp bases out of found objects and vintage lamps. The look is rustic, Western, cottage, modern, Victorian and eclectic!

Catherine Miles

French Influence

Marburger Farm: *Tent A*
Zapp Hall Antique Show

Pensacola Beach, Florida
c. 404.784.3442
frenchinfluence@bellsouth.net

Murielle Abeger

*F*rench Influence focuses on French antiques and decorative accessories. The owner, Murielle Abeger, has been frequenting the flea markets in Paris since she was a young girl. She is known especially for her painted French furniture and is an avid collector of Murano glass.

Q: *What's your favorite Round Top story?*

A: I once had a customer with real diamonds on her cowboy boots!

Q: *What's the most unusual thing you've ever sold?*

A: A hairdressing chair made with horns and cowhide.

J Hill Designs

Marburger Farm: *Tent A*

т. 903.984.1487
с. 903.983.0898
www.jhilldesigns.net

3041 FM 2276
Kilgore, Texas 75662

I buy and sell antiques with a passion for "cottage style." To complement our antiques I designed our line of soft goods, "Whitewashed," which has a relaxed feel and a vintage look. In addition, we offer custom styling and design.

My area of expertise is my ability to take a piece of furniture that is tattered, faded, worn and sometimes broken and use it as-is to make a beautiful statement.

Judy Hill

Q&A

Q: What inspired you to start your business?

A: My passion to create, along with my encouragement from family and friends.

Q: What advice would you give to the shoppers at Round Top?

A: Don't make a list! If you see it and love it, you'd better buy it or it will be gone before you get back.

Q: What is the one thing everyone should do (besides shop!) while at the Round Top Antiques Show?

A: Take country roadtrips.

Q: What's your favorite part of the "Round Top Experience"?

A: Creating a different look each time I design a booth.

Jerry Earnhardt Antiques

Marburger Farm: *Tent C*

3626 South Dixie Highway
West Palm Beach, Florida 33405
T. 561.531.0426
Jerry Earnhardt, *Owner*

*J*erry Earnhardt specializes exclusively in Italian antiques, focusing on smalls, sconces and chandeliers. He conducts buying trips throughout the year to fill his two warehouses with beautiful items, and focuses on sales to the trade. In addition to Marburger Farm, where he has been showing for about 10 years, Jerry exhibits each year in Atlanta.

Q: *What is your favorite part of the "Round Top Experience"?*

A: I love Texas and I think Marburger Farm is the best market there.

Queenie Tin & Mirror Co. specializes in beautifully distressed vintage mirrors from the 1850's to the 1940's. I also offer unique home accessories handmade from antique ceiling tin and architectural findings. I choose only pieces that have the most beautiful, original paint. All of my offerings have a lovely, old-world feel. The palette is always soft, ranging from whites and creams to those wonderful verdis gris hues.

Queenie Tin & Mirror Co.

Lisa A. McQueen

Marburger Farm: *Tent C*

9341 East Sugar Grove Drive
Terre Haute, Indiana 47803
т. 812.236.5911
msqueen99@aol.com
www.queenietin.com

Q&A

Q: What else do we need to know?

A: I want all of my clients and potential clients to know that I *love* what I do and feel it's reflected in my work.

Q: What is your favorite thing to do during the show?

A: Prom Night Party but also just admiring the stars at night in that big ol' Texas sky!

Richards Antiques

Hugh E. Richards

Marburger Farm: *Tent F*

P. O. Box 780693
Wichita, Kansas 67278
T. 316.371.7262
H. 316.682.7502
hughrich1@sbcglobal.net

Hugh Richards has been a collector his entire life. He "sold the bank" in 1982, owned an antiques store for 11 years, and has been doing antiques shows ever since. He specializes in Lalique and Sabino art glass, sterling silver salt spoons, old handmade and machine-made marbles, and hard-to-find sterling silver items.

Roberts Antiques

Marburger Farm: *Tent F*
EX·CESS

Homer, Michigan
T. 407.342.6804
H. 352.409.7662
mijoantiques@aol.com

We have a very eclectic look and a wide variety ranging from fine French and Italian furniture and smalls to garden statuary, urns and wicker. We carry something for everyone's tastes and budgets, whether you are doing a room, garden, or a whole house. We buy and sell the things that we love and would want to live with in our own home.

Jodie & Mike Roberts

Q: *What inspired you to start your business?*

A: Having both families in the antiques business, it was in our blood and inevitable that we too would be in the business!

JEWELED
MADONNA'S
CROWN
IN EXCELLENT
CONDITION
c.1880
$1,100 ea

GILDED
...ATEAU
1870

#215

We spend three months a year in France to find truly special pieces. We work hard in bustling French markets and places undiscovered by Americans to unearth the rare and unusual at affordable prices. It's our passion. The French aesthetic is elegant and effortless. The wonderful old religious pieces speak of history and emotion, creating an environment of comfort and opulence. It's the French way.

Jessica & David Fairbrother

Q: What inspired you to start your business?

A: 1) Desire to use the French learned in school. 2) Needed to get out of the country for extended periods. 3) Mall security cop job was taken. 4) Serious addiction to the hunt for antiques.

Q: What's the most unusual thing you've ever sold?

A: The Holy Grail (it could have been just an old wooden cup).

Q: What inspired you to be a vendor at Round Top?

A: We were missing all the fun!

Vintage Sculpture

Brad & Sundie Ruppert

Marburger Farm: *Tent G,*
The Artisan Tent

T. 515.981.5189
C. 515.991.6083
vintagesculpture@studiogonline.com
www.vintagesculpture.com

*U*sing a wide variety of vintage, found, recycled and repurposed treasures, we create original and often whimsical assemblage sculptures. We believe that life should be lived passionately and you should surround yourself with things you love and that make you smile… this is very obvious in the artwork we create!

Q&A

Q: *What inspired you to start your business?*

A: Our son's 2nd grade project! We had to make a turkey as a family and when he turned his project in, he took five orders from teachers and parents! It just grew from there! Later, a friend suggested we contact Miss Emma Lee Turney to show at her Folk Art Tent.

Q: *What is your favorite part of the "Round Top Experience"?*

A: One of the things that we love most about Round Top is the "community" that gathers every six months. It is so much more than just an antiques show! It's friends, family, buying, selling, living and laughing. It's an amazing little phenomenom that happens in those cow pastures, and we feel blessed to be able to live that life twice a year and consider ourselves fortunate to be surrounded by kindred spirits.

Willow Nest

◦ Marburger Farm: *Tent A*

T. 360.835.9023
lindamarcov@yahoo.com
www.willownest.net

701 North Main Street
Burton, Texas 77835

Willow Nest is known for having a soft, romantic palette, with a strong influence of European elements. Ludmil, an accomplished welder, often takes items in need of serious repair and re-creates them, as in a French alter or aviary. His passion is gardening, so a birdbath or an old cart would not be unusual in our booth. Linda is a true romantic and it shows in all she presents.

Ludmil & Linda Marcov

Q&A

Q: *What inspired you to start your business?*

A: The love of the discarded item, the desire to use and enjoy pieces that have had a long and purposeful life in many homes … believing in the value of using what you have.

Q: *What's your favorite part of the "Round Top Experience"?*

A: We love watching it unfold right before our eyes, all the details coming together all around us, teams of people working together to bring the customer the finest, most desirable, and unique things.

Q: *What do you specialize in?*

A: Textiles, French farmhouse and garden, old Paris elements, and wedding collections.

Antiques Show Venue

The Original Round Top Antiques Fair

т. 512.237.4747
т. 979.278.3513 *show week only*
info@roundtoptexasantiques.com
www.roundtoptexasantiques.com

475 South Highway 237
Round Top, Texas 78932
Susan & Bo Franks, *Owners*

The Original Round Top Antiques Fair is the antiques show that started the entire Round Top–Warrenton phenomenon about forty-three years ago. The many-miles-long array of antiques shows and shops is an outgrowth of the Round Top Antiques Fair. From its beginning, with only 22 superb dealers in tiny Rifle Hall, this show continues to uphold its excellent reputation. We feature the highest-quality antiques, in all price ranges, in four venues at the Big Red Barn Event Center and Carmine Dance Hall. We are, indeed, proud to be the owners of this prestigious and always-exciting show.

Susan Franks

Q&A

Q: *What other services/amenities do you offer?*

A: Our buildings and the Continental Tent are air-conditioned, and we have plenty of free parking and a free shuttle between the Carmine Dance Hall and the Big Red Barn. We have clean, air-conditioned restrooms plus porters and shippers on-site to assist our customers. We serve award-winning barbecue at Carmine Dance Hall, and Royers Round Top Café is the food concessionaire at the Big Red Barn.

Q: *What is your favorite part of the "Round Top Experience"?*

A: My absolute favorite is opening morning! Hundreds of customers line up at the entrance before starting time. They are excited and literally run through the doors. After the many hours we spend setting up to make the show perfect, this fervor gives us new energy — energy that carries us all the way through to the end of the show.

Suzy Smith Antiques & Interiors

The Original Round Top Antiques Fair: *White Tent at Big Red Barn*

т. 832.444.1230
т. 713.522.6996
londoncowboys@mac.com

at Antiques & Interiors
on Dunlavy
3845 Dunlavy Street
Houston, Texas 77079

Suzy Smith

Inspired by my first trip to Paris, I created a business focusing on a variety of French and English antiques. I love buying vintage textiles and lighting. My area of expertise includes brocante and the creative application of vintage fabrics. I have always been inspired by history, and love being able to source pieces of the past.

~Q&A~

Q: *What is your background?*

A: I have a fine arts degree from Trinity College, as well as a degree in fashion design from Washington University in St. Louis. I also attended Parsons School of Design in Paris. I had my own clothing and handbag lines and later became a stylist, working on several catalog sets for Neiman Marcus, Horchow and Pier One. While living in London, I worked as a contributing editor for *Mary Engelbreit's Home Companion* magazine, producing and styling a number of their UK features.

Antiques Show Venue

Sterling McCall
Antiques Showcase & Event Center

c. 832.671.7821
kj@johnstonandco.com
www.sterlingmccallantiques-events.com

Highway 237
Warrenton, Texas 78954
Kathy Johnston, *Manager*

This new antiques showcase in the heart of Warrenton offers a wide variety of premium-quality antique items in a museum-like setting. Everything from antique crystal to Civil–war era guns, vintage clothing, classic jukeboxes, fine estate jewelry and stunning furniture both primitive and classic, make the Sterling McCall Antiques Showcase a must-see location for serious shoppers who wish to browse in complete comfort.

Q&A

Q: *What can shoppers expect to find at your venue?*

A: An eclectic array of the highest quality true antiques. No reproductions are allowed and all dealers are juried into the show.

Q: *What services and amenities do you offer?*

A: Entrance to the show is free, and limited, paved parking is available for $5 per car. A U.S. post office is right on-site so shipping smaller items is easy. Bistro 108, La Grange's top-rated restaurant, is our exclusive food service provider.

Antiques Show Venue

Texas Rose Show

Vickie Davis

2075 Highway 237
Round Top, Texas 78954
T. 256.390.5337
info@texasroseshow.com
www.texasroseshow.com

*T*exas Rose Show is a bi-annual antiques show that offers a wide variety of goods and services in a 3600-square-foot building on five acres of spacious property for vendors and shoppers. The show offers a myriad of antique items including industrial items, architectural pieces, fine china, primitive furniture, linens, and works of art.

Q&A

Q: *What services do you offer?*

A: Texas Rose Show offers camping, food and drink services, restrooms, free parking and admission, and an optional delivery service. The show is open late Monday night to accommodate late shoppers. Our venue can also host accommodate private events.

Q: *What are you passionate about collecting?*

A: Lace and 18th Century sterling perfume bottles.

Q: *What's the most unusual thing you've ever sold?*

A: Georg Jensen's thirteenth piece of silver jewelry to be put on display at the Georg Jensen museum in Denmark.

Duchess D

T. 904.501.4721
theduchess@duchessd.com
www.duchessd.com

334 East 10th Street
Jacksonville, Florida 32206

◦ Texas Rose Show

*D*uchess D is where necessity greets luxury. The Duchess offers a playful mix of all things unique, fun and useful. Duchess D follows the same mantra when selling, blogging, tweeting, or simply being. It simply means this: Buy the things you love. Mix periods, styles and colors. Layer, layer, layer. And most importantly, believe in yourself and your vision.

Debbie Freeman, *The Duchess*

Q: *What is your area of expertise?*

A: The Duchess D collection ranges from classically tasteful to outlandishly thoughtful. Pieces from the collection will fit in any interior: traditional, industrial, mid-century modern, Danish modern, retro, Hollywood Regency, or an eclectic mix!

Q: *What is your favorite part of the "Round Top Experience"?*

A: I love the passion of buyers and dealers alike. We all endure the elements for the Round Top experience.

Q: *What inspired you to start your business?*

A: The Duchess embarked on a career in art and antiques to assist her clients in crafting a design language of their own.

Antiques Show Venue

Zapp Hall Antique Show

т. 713.824.1157
c. 713.560.7265
т. 979.249.3657 *show week only*
info@zapphall.com
www.zapphall.com

4217 South Highway 237
Warrenton, Texas 78961
Cheryl Lehane & Karen McCord

From fine European antiquities that "talk" to the seasoned collector and preposterously pink lions perfect for livening up the living room, to hot hip-swinging honky-tonk, succulent sirloin or shrimp suppers and French Champagne toasts, Zapp Hall Antique Show is the most divinely diverse event in all of Warrenton. Our motto is "Come for the antiques, stay for the atmosphere"— quite an atmosphere it is!

Not only are the antiques unparalleled, but as the Junk Gypsies explain, "The soul of the show is uplifting and inspiring." Mouthwatering food, cold beer and exquisite Champagne sets Zapp Hall apart.

Q&A

Q: *What inspired you to start your business?*

A: The Zapp Hall Antique Show is run by four generations of the Evans family. Only the second owners of the property, Bud and Carolyn Evans decided more than 20 years ago to bolster the Warrenton community.

Q: *What other events take place at your venue throughout the year?*

A: Weddings, family reunions, and private parties.

Q: *What is your favorite part of the "Round Top Experience"?*

A: The magical part of the Round Top Experience lies in the relationships that are forged that extend far beyond the show … it is a reunion of kindred spirits and polar opposites … it is a highlight in the journey of life that can only be explained through "experience!"

ANTIQUES AND SO MUCH MORE!

While the dealers of the Zapp Hall Antique Show offer jaw-dropping, eye-popping vignettes of epic proportions, the shopping is but a piece of the pie! Speaking of "pie," don't miss Royers Cafe's world-famous homemade pies after you dine on quail, shrimp and tenderloin in the Zapp Hall Beer Garden. From toe-tapping Texas music and ice-cold beers to the soulful sounds of the Harbor Light Choir of the Salvation Army, from the famous frozen cappucino to the sparkling, French bubbly of the Bubble Lounge Champagne Bar, the Zapp Hall Antique Show is antiques and so much *more*... it is a destination that is sure to satisfy all the senses!

Zapp Hall

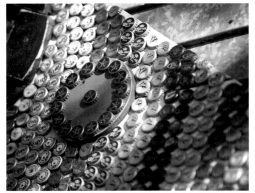

In addition to the vast array of treasures you'll find while shopping the Zapp Hall Antique Show, we offer lunch and dinner, live music in the beer garden and the Bubble Lounge at Zapp Hall.

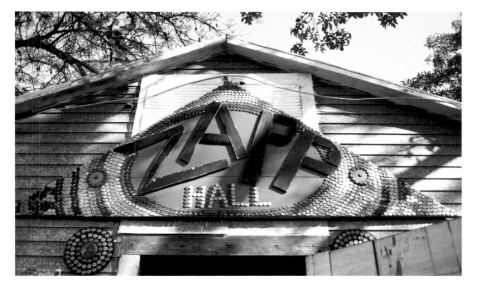

-Q&A-

Q: *What is your favorite thing to do during the show?*

A: Toast friends, old and new, in the Bubble Lounge while sharing stories of the "finds of the day!"

Q: *What is the one thing everyone should do (besides shop!) while in Round Top?*

A: Cool off during the day with a famous frozen cappucino from the Zapp Hall concession stand. And spend an evening enjoying live music under the stars in the Zapp Hall Beer (and wine!) Garden and Bubble Lounge Champagne Bar.

Dead People's Stuff &
Grandma Had It Antiques

◦ Zapp Hall Antique Show

т. 405.275.7766
c. 405.566.9066 *Glenita*
c. 405.517.3987 *Shirley*
deadpeoplesstuff1955@yahoo.com

33670 West Old Highway 270
Shawnee, Oklahoma 74804

We specialize in Great American primitives, original-paint and refinished items, old mercantile pieces, Western items, old tools, art, quilts, stoneware crocks, estate items and vintage garden pieces. Our original shop located 30 miles east of Oklahoma City is an old Victorian house, and we have added several buildings and a couple of barns over the years, all full of antiques, plants, flowers and other garden items.

Shirley & Glenita Hayden

Q&A

Q: *What inspired you to start your business?*

A: I fell in love with a beautiful, heavy iron and brass bed, held my first garage sale to pay for it, and thus started the vicious cycle of being an antiques dealer!

Q: *What is your favorite Round Top story?*

A: Twenty-some years ago my daughter was set up in Warrenton and her father and I were coming from a show back East. We stopped to see her, unloaded what we had left, and we all ended up selling all we had *and* the truck we brought it in! Had to ride back with her — good times!

Q: *What are you passionate about collecting?*

A: Primitive furniture, stoneware, and Texas bluebonnet paintings.

Junk Gypsy

° Zapp Hall Antique Show

т. 979.776.5151
junkgypsy@gypsyville.com
www.gypsyville.com

4345 Alexis Court
College Station, Texas 77845

$\mathcal{G}$ ypsyville is the raucous and rowdy home of gypsies, junkers, dreamers, and true-blue rebels across the globe! We believe every man's trash is our treasure, junking is a bonafide sport, and garage sales are our Mall of America. We'd rather be outside in the middle of the country at a flea market collecting chippy-peely castoffs than scooping up the latest cashmere sweater at Neiman's once-a-year sale.

Owners Janie Sikes, Jolie Sikes-Smith & Amie Sikes
with husband / father Phillip Sikes

Q&A

Q: *What is your favorite part of the "Round Top Experience"?*

A: Several years ago, a tornado (aka a Texas twister) was looming on the outskirts of town. The sheriff came to our tent and warned us and the line of customers that everyone needed to evacuate the tent immediately and find a safe spot to ride out the storm. After the storm, when we returned to the tent, we found several stacks of money on the counter and hand-written receipts ... our never-say-die customers had weathered the storm shopping!

Q: *What era style are you known for?*

A: We combine chippy-peely flea market furniture and elegant chandeliers with a little bit of hippie Texas flair, some southern-fried cowgirl pride and a splash of Moulin Rouge eccentricity to achieve the Junk Gypsy look.

Q: *What tip would you give to new collectors?*

A: Sometimes the stories behind each piece are the most valuable part of the collection.

JUNKOLOGY 101

- Wear comfortable shoes.
- Pack extra cash.
  (Some vendors don't take plastic.)
- Wear sunscreen and pack rain gear.
  (Remember this is Texas, people!)
- Grab a *Show Daily* for maps and vital vendor info.
- Be a kind negotiator.
- Drink a cold beer at Zapp Hall.
- Don't forget to take a souvenir pic in the Junk Gypsy outhouse!

Junk Gypsy

*O*ur design philosophy is completely across the board but it all comes together in a look that is truly JUNK GYPSY, in all its cluttered, tattered, saturated glory! We believe in decadent junk and *fun*, spirited styles coming together to create a space that defines who you are.

Q: *How did you start your business?*

A: In 1998 we shucked the world of convention. With $2000, a beat-up pickup truck, *big dreams* and a whole lotta blood, sweat and tears we began the journey of a lifetime!

Q: *What inspired you to be a vendor at Round Top?*

A: We'd always heard it was the Promised Land for antiques and really good junk!

"Junk has energy! If you're not feeling the good energy vibes, don't buy it!" — *The Famous Joe Pete*

WHAT KEEPS YOU COMING BACK TO ROUND TOP?

"We have been doing this for 30 years and have yet to tire of it, and we find ourselves excited before each show and ready to set up our magic and see friends that we sometimes only see twice a year at shows … both vendors and customers."

LINDA & LUDMIL MARCOV, Willow Nest

"We have a lot of fun making our stuff and traveling around the country. We always stop to look for new and interesting things and get a lot of great ideas on our trips to sell our handmade stuff. We always have Round Top in mind for anything we find that we think is great."

KATHY & DON GROSS, Austin Woodhenge

"Being an antiques dealer is not easy. When you do it right, it's not a job, it's more of an all-consuming lifestyle. But it is truly a privilege to be able to do what you love and share it with your friends.

JESSICA & DAVID FAIRBROTHER,
Sacred Heart Antiques

"The sense of freedom it gives me and the pleasure I get from meeting people. I want all of my clients and potential clients to know that *I love* what I do and feel it's reflected in my work."

LISA A. McQUEEN, Queenie Tin & Mirror Co

"We absolutely love what we do and cannot imagine doing anything else."

JODIE & MIKE ROBERTS, Roberts Antiques

"Showing at Round Top gives us a chance to get to know our customers, an experience we miss by being in multi-dealer locations where we are not always present. We can find out what people are looking for, so when we go to France we can look for items for specific customers. We have met such interesting people from all over the country, both shoppers and other dealers. We always look forward to seeing our Round Top friends!"

MARTHA & DAVID PARNELL, Brocante

"Interacting with friends and vendors and finding new dealers to buy from. Of course we are all looking for that treasure that will become the find of a lifetime, but that is part of the fun of it."

KATHY JOHNSON, Pieces of the Past

"My favorite part of coming to Round Top would definitely be getting to see all of our wonderful clients that became very good friends over the years and, of course, the dinners at Royers and the great bunch of dealers — they are amazing people!

ENDER TASCI, Elephant Walk Interiors & Antiques

Wayne Ayers Folk Art

I create Folk Art sculptures, whirligigs, and weathervane forms based on 18th, 19th and 20th Century originals plus many pieces that stem directly from my imagination. I also buy and sell antiques, including early blown glass and primitive to high country furniture with an emphasis on surface and early paint finishes. I do commission pieces in a variety of mediums — weathervanes, folk art sculpture, wall hangings, etc. On occasion and as time allows, I also repair and restore antique furniture and folk art pieces.

Wayne Ayers

Emma Lee Turney's Folk Art Fair and Creative Market: *Highway 237 North of downtown Round Top*

4309 Wonder Hill Road
Chappell Hill, Texas 77426
T. 252.452.1231
C. 970.270.1277
kayers6@yahoo.com

CONTRIBUTING
PHOTOGRAPHERS

Casey Woods Photography

Casey Woods Maddeaux

Austin, Texas
т. 512.576.5918
casey@caseywoods.com
www.caseywoods.com

Casey's work has been featured in the *Austin Design Guide, Rare Magazine, CRAVE Austin,* and various ad campaigns.

*C*asey Woods is an editorial and commercial photographer based in Austin. Her work has appeared in galleries, magazines, and advertising campaigns throughout the state.

Q: *What is your area of expertise?*

A: At heart I'm a storyteller. From residential interiors to portraits, I enjoy working with each client to thoroughly illustrate their ideas and concepts.

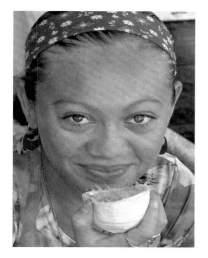

Deb Did It

160 Heritage Street
P.O. Box 284
Carmine, Texas 78932
T. 979.830.7866
heritagehaus@yahoo.com
www.debdiditphotography.blogspot.com

Nothing gives me more pleasure as a photographer than when a person opens up and allows me to capture their true spirit in a natural setting. I love to take pictures every single day of random moments that are unexpected, which could include a broken egg on the floor, laundry on the line or a project in my sewing machine.

Q: *Do you offer any additional services, features or activities?*

A: I sell sets of notecards with my photographs. A popular item at artisan bazaars!

Deb Taylor

Deb's work has been featured in the *Women of Round Top* calendar, *Creative Cups for the Cause* calendar, *Texas Live*, *Somerset Studios*, *Cloth-Paper-Scissors* and *Flair*.

Diane Mueller Photography

Diane Mueller

La Grange, Texas
T. 979.733.3092
T. 979.725.8812
dianek@txun.net
www.dianemuellerphoto.com

*D*iane Mueller is a portrait photographer working indoors and outdoors. She specializes in photographing high school seniors, children, families and weddings. Patience and flexibility are her greatest virtues.

Q: *What inspired you to start your business?*

A: I discovered my love for photography more than 25 years ago. I can't imagine doing anything else. I find photography very rewarding and today's technology very intriguing.

La Dolce Vita Photography

Austin, Texas
T. 512.608.8000
alina@ladolcevitaphoto.com
www.ladolcevitaphoto.com

La Dolce Vita Photography is a boutique photography studio located in Austin. We are passionate about creating distinctly fine art lifestyle photography for your wedding or your business. We welcome commissions around the world and love photographing people and beautiful locations.

Alina Prax

Alina's work has been featured in *The Austin Statesman, Greener Photography, Tribeza* and on Forbes.com and Austin360.com

Otto Helweg Photography

Otto Helweg

Austin, Texas
T. 512.595.3665
otto@ottomatic.com
www.ottomatic.com

*O*tto's professional work typically focuses on interior photography for residential real estate and high-end homes, following Michael Harris' methodology. Presently his personal projects include capturing people interacting within their social environments or public places. More specifically, he's currently working on mastering low-light environments for Austin's music scene. Otto's work is typically shot with a single light source or outside the studio with natural light.

Q Weddings

Suzi Q

I travel worldwide to photograph weddings with unique decor, artisanal food presentation and innovative tablescapes. Besides my detail shots, I'm also known for documenting important moments as well as creating timeless portraits. I photograph life, but prettier.

Q: *What is your area of expertise?*

A: I shoot film (it is so beautiful). Two things I'm known for: my imagery of details (food, flowers, collectibles, shoes, etc.) and simple, authentic portraits. I'm quite experienced as a traveling photographer.

T. 512.944.8331
suzi@qweddings.com
www.qweddings.com

Suzi Q's images have been published in: *Exquisite Weddings, The Knot* (Texas, New York, California, Michigan), *Conde Nast Brides of Northern California, The Sun* and in these books: *Surreal Gourmet Bites, Kirtsy Takes a Bow, Crave Austin,* and *Spectacular Weddings of Texas.*

Vanityfire Photography

Shanti Matulewski

915 North Lamar Boulevard
Austin, Texas 78703
т. 512.970.3095
vanityfirephotography@gmail.com
www.vanityfire.com

*V*anityfire Photography specializes in personal or promotional portraiture with creative staging and execution, satisfying and comfortable client relationships and unique photographic processes and printing. Vanityfire Photography exhibits a fluidity and ease in dealing with the subject, and this extends to the resulting images.

Q: *What do you specialize in?*

A: My artwork depicting feminine, ethereal, and dreamlike images. I have experience printing on alternative materials to create a work of art from a simple portrait. I also have a woodworker on retainer that builds custom frames and light boxes.

Notes

ALPHABETICAL INDEX

INDEX TO LOCAL BUSINESSES & ATTRACTIONS BY TOWN

INDEX TO ANTIQUES SHOWS BY VENUE

Gretchen von Rochow & Kerry Rupp